ISBN 978-1-331-04271-6
PIBN 10137378

English
Français
Deutsche
Italiano
Español
Português

www.forgottenbooks.com

Mythology Photography **Fiction**
Fishing Christianity **Art** Cooking
Essays Buddhism Freemasonry
Medicine **Biology** Music **Ancient
Egypt** Evolution Carpentry Physics
Dance Geology **Mathematics** Fitness
Shakespeare **Folklore** Yoga Marketing
Confidence Immortality Biographies
Poetry **Psychology** Witchcraft
Electronics Chemistry History **Law**
Accounting **Philosophy** Anthropology
Alchemy Drama Quantum Mechanics
Atheism Sexual Health **Ancient History**
Entrepreneurship Languages Sport
Paleontology Needlework Islam
Metaphysics Investment Archaeology
Parenting Statistics Criminology
Motivational

SAMUEL S. MITCHELL, D.D.

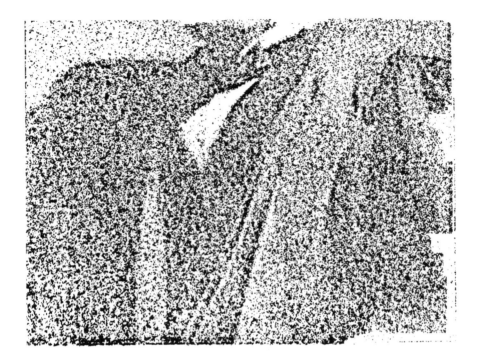

The Presbyterian Pulpit

---·✳·---

THE STAFF METHOD

BY THE

REV. S. S. MITCHELL, D. D.

Pastor of the First Presbyterian Church, Buffalo, N. Y.

PHILADELPHIA

PRESBYTERIAN BOARD OF PUBLICATION
AND SABBATH-SCHOOL WORK

1904

CONTENTS

THE STAFF METHOD

THE STAFF METHOD

I

THE STAFF METHOD

"The child is not awaked."—2 KINGS iv : 31.

DOING good by indirection, at arm's length, through a substitute, by a check—the impersonal staff method is in danger of being overworked in our day.

Notice, I pray you, a familiar type of this impersonalism upon the lower level, that you may be prepared to recognize it upon the higher. When the man first commenced business he was accustomed to see everyone who called. But with the growth of his business, and the increase of his power and fame, this simple and direct meeting with his individual patrons came to an end. Now, if you will call at the man's office, unless your business is of the first importance and you yourself somebody in particular, you will see nothing of the head of the firm. First the doorkeeper sifts; then the head clerk sifts; then the junior partner sifts; and only the elect can penetrate to the inner sanctum, upon the closed door of which stare the letters of the word " Private." Personality has vanished from the public office, leaving an impersonal mechanism in its place. From the inner office, three rooms deep from the street, the great man sends his staff to do the work that comes unto him.

Time was when the poor woman who brought her child in her arms, or the laboring man who could only get to the office after six o'clock in the evening, was met by the doctor himself, who by a personal interest in their cases, and by a personal attention to their necessities, did them more good than all his medicines. But now practice has increased; fame has come; a sense of power and greatness has waxed strong; and as a result all ordinary cases must be turned over to the assistant. No doubt there is a necessity compelling unto this state of things. Brain-power, heart-power, nerve-power,—no man can give without limitation these precious and remedial forces to those who have need. Let us then lift up no voice of criticism or fault-finding. Instead, let us quietly take our seat in the outer office and wait our turn to see the assistant, and then as quietly come away with the assurance that we have received all we had a right to expect. To be sure, the man himself did not see us, but the office did. We had the benefit of the staff.

Now these common pictures to be seen upon every side of us are not a bad representation of that which has come to be a common occurrence in the moral world. When he himself was weak and unknown, the man kept his Sunday class in the Mission School. But when success came and prosperity; when the man, through development, became a power in the community, he withdrew from the ranks of the Mission workers, compelling the drafting in of a new and weaker substitute. Now the man sends his check regularly once a year, but he himself no longer knows the way unto the Mission.

When the woman's time was as plentiful as it was cheap, she used some of it in visits of personal condolence and sympathy. Now, however, since her husband has become wealthy and she herself a leader in society, she has given up all such personal service. Instead, now she sends a bundle of clothing, or some jelly, or a gift of money.

Now it may have been something like this which happened in the case of Elisha. Suddenly, with the departure of Elijah, he had blossomed into a full-grown prophet, walking the earth as if hand in hand with the Infinite One, and doing wonderful works of mercy and of power. With this new importance and with the great multiplication of his daily cares and duties, it would not be strange if the prophet came unto an undue sense of the importance of his personality and unto the conviction that he could not afford to give his personal attention unto every case of need that presented itself. So when the poor Shunammite appeared before him, he cried out: "Her child is sick, her child is sick; run, Gehazi, with my staff." Or he may have thought, as the great physician seems sometimes to conclude concerning his office, "Everything connected with me, everything belonging to the great prophet, is full of virtue; run, Gehazi, with my staff." But whatever was the feeling or conviction which led to its use, the staff method did not prove a success in Elisha's case.

"And Gehazi passed on before them, and laid the staff upon the face of the child; but there was neither voice, nor hearing." Immediately the prophet's proxy turns back unto his master with this announcement of failure: "The child is not awaked, the child is not awaked." Oh, Elisha! great as thou art, thy staff is not yet sufficient to do thy work in the world. Thou thyself also art needed.

But let us turn from these introductory thoughts unto the direct consideration of the subject thus brought before us. I indicate two general lines for the guidance of your thought :—

First. The faultiness of the staff method.

Secondly. The requisitions which evermore issue for the presence of the person.

The first prominent fault of the staff method is this: It is a withholding of that which is the finest and grandest power of the human life. The human mind or spirit possesses a mysterious power of reaching the human mind and spirit. So evident is this that some, as Sir William Thomson, have gone so far as to call this power the sixth sense. The living man wields a power that his words do not possess and which his agent cannot carry with him or exercise. When Daniel Webster rose from his seat at the dinner-table although frequently he said but little, and that little commonplace, the whole company felt his power. It was the force of his personality which bore them down. Men act upon this principle in all secular matters of first importance. When a business transaction of great magnitude is to be determined, the telegram is not sent, or

the letter written, or the confidential clerk dis-
patched, but the man goes himself. Yet not
always do men so act in the field of moral service. The banker says : "This is to be a busy
day with me. I wish you would send to the City
Missionary and have her call upon that poor
family of whom we were speaking, and tell her
if she will come to my office on her way I will
give her a check." The woman says : "Every
hour of my day is taken up. It will be impossible for me to make the visit to Mrs. A. that I
had purposed. I am sorry for this, for I hear the
poor woman is in great affliction over the loss of
her husband. Still, I will endeavor to send her
some articles of clothing, of which I hear she is
greatly in need."

So also the inferior life is sent as a substitute,
as well as the check or the bundle of clothing.
The man draws out of the charity board or the
mission when he is in the full bloom of his personal power, saying, as he does so, "I must con-
tent myself, for the future, to work by proxy in
those needy fields." So men and women send
the staff to do the Lord's work instead of going
themselves, and in so doing hold back from moral
service the finest power that they possess. It is
in man, what Jesus Christ had been guilty of if

He had sent to our world a book, or a messenger, instead of coming Himself.

Another fault inhering in the staff method is its non-recognition of soul life in those who are to be served. There is no law more fundamental than this—"God has made of one blood all nations of men for to dwell upon all the face of the earth." Or, as Jesus Christ puts it—"One is your Master, and all ye are brethren." The ignorant are so many darkened souls; the hungry are human souls in a starving body; the human need that cries out for help is the cry of a human spirit. Now, the sending of the money-staff or the old-clothes-staff is a non-recognition of these souls, and by this fact the sending must be adjudged as poor and imperfect. I remember very well that the giving of money or of anything else is not so impulsive, or widespread, or general as to render necessary any words to be spoken against it. Such words I am not speaking. All that I affirm is that the giving of things cannot fill out the measure of obligation that we owe to living souls. Often what the unfortunates need more than money is a new endowment of moral force. They need the reëstablishment of their self-respect; the joy of a new hope; the tonic, the inspiration of a new courage, and these necessities cannot be

passed to them in the shape of a check. Only
life in personal contact can beget life. Only love
can inspire love. Only souls can breathe new
life into souls.

But let us pass to the more important part of
our subject—the authoritative requisitions that
evermore issue for the presence, in the field of
human need, of the person.

The first of these issues in the name of charity.
Sweet Charity she is sometimes called, although
this pet name, it is to be feared, is sometimes given
her by those who strangely confound the odorless
character of her serene majesty with the more
earthly sweetness that diffuses itself throughout
the Ball which, without any very good authority,
is dedicated to her name. The requisition here
issues for the protection, for the defense, of
charity. Giving, from which personal knowledge
and personal administration are excluded, is apt
to do more harm than good. The Charity Or-
ganization Society of New York, after the investigation of thousands of cases, gives out the
conclusion that, of all applications for aid, less
than one in sixteen require continuous help, and
less than one in four needs even temporary aid.
Many a pauper, it adds, is found upon investigation to be without the necessaries of life in the

public gaze, but privately in full possession of its luxuries. The Rev. S. A. Barnett, founder of Toynbee Hall, after a wide experience and observation, declares that it is well-nigh impossible to give to people what they ask for without doing them a serious injury. The conclusion, therefore, would seem to be inevitable that unless we are willing that charity should be turned into a failure and farce; unless we are willing to offer her gifts as a premium upon laziness and lying; unless we are ready to convert her heart into a trough, into which the swine of hypocrisy and dead-beatism shall thrust both feet and snout; unless we are willing to have her fair form pilloried before the eyes of the community as an evil-doer, there must walk with her through the field of human need the person who is to give unto this need. It is sadly and evermore true that many of the world's most necessitous lives, those who are struggling against the direst poverty, must be hunted out. These persons do not parade their necessity, but make the most ingenious and pathetic attempts to conceal it. Many of them starve, or freeze, or commit suicide rather than beg. Take the terrible truth here in a single sentence as Henry George has written it down: "In the richest city of the world the mortuary reports contain a column for deaths by starvation." Now, such grim results are possible in that city and other cites, not because of the lack of human and Christian sympathy, but because there is a lack of knowledge, and there is this lack of knowledge because so few of the liberal and the charitable make any personal investigation in the field of human needs. Therefore charity sends forth in her own beautiful name the requisition for the person of the giver. The staff will not answer here. What is wanted is, that the kindly, and loving, and giving soul, shall itself go unto the discovery of the poverty which it is so willing to receive. The result of this shall be not only to protect charity from the abuses which now discredit her fair fame and spoil her usefulness, but will also quicken with new enthusiasm her beautiful life. The first requisition here issues in the name that is reverenced by all mankind, the name of charity, the sweet daughter of God.

A second requisition for the person of the good-doer issues in the name of faith, of faith that through all the days of time walks our earth as charity's twin sister. That men may see your good works, and—what? Do what? Rejoice in your benefactions? Come unto comfort and confidence through your kindness and help? Lift up their praises to crown your head? No; not any of these things. That "men . . . may see your good works, and glorify your Father which is in heaven"; that men may see your goodness and believe in the infinite goodness. This faith-producing power is the crowning glory of human beneficence. To teach men God—to lead them unto the belief of the divine—this is the finest inspiration, and this the richest reward that waits for and crowns the serving life. For consider that the hungry body that is to-day fed, and the naked one that is to-day clothed, will soon pass beyond the possibility of these sensations—lie as so much dust in a little grave, to be hungry or cold no more. The mind that to-day wanders in darkness will soon break through its unfriendly barriers into the eternal light. The heart that aches to-day and breaks to-day passes quickly forward unto the end of its woe. "There the wicked cease from troubling; and there the weary are at rest." The starving mother who, in the year 1890, with her baby in her arms threw herself off the Hoboken dock, to-day can look back and say, "It was a grim moment for baby and me, that splash and clasp of the dark waters—but that was all over long ago." No, not in any end bound up with the life of this mortal body, not in any momentary relief from sentient suffering can be found the highest motive and the enduring reward of human beneficence. This fact makes the giving of self an indispensable condition of true Christian service. The man of the world, after he has grown enormously rich, writes out his check for a Free Library, or a University Professorship, or a magnificent church edifice. But this act of his has little power to convince a selfish and unbelieving world. Men will say that this is only so much restitution. They will scoff at the act as an offered atonement—an attempt, through the use of a moiety of selfishly acquired riches, to purchase standing here and a place in heaven. In the sense of which we are speaking no money gift can reach unto the supreme end of human service, for it does not certify the existence of disinterested love. As James Russell Lowell has strongly said, the only conclusive evidence of a man's sincerity is that he gives himself. Words, money, all things else, are easily given. But when a man makes a gift of himself it is plain to all that the truth has taken possession of him. When Governor Washburne, of Massachusetts, found time in, or took time from, his official duties weekly to visit the sick and the

poor of his native village, kindly to speak to and
to pray with them, he thus brought the Divine
love into the sphere of their vision—he thus led
them in the direction of faith by the sweet per-
suasion of a Power which human nature is unable
to resist.

We may as well recognize the fact, my fellow-
men, that a new day in the history of the world is
upon us. Do you say it is a very restless, selfish,
lawless, devilish day? Yes, no doubt it is something of all of these. Nevertheless it is with us this
day and we are in it—a day when the unfortunate
and the poor and the suffering can no longer be
persuaded nor charmed unto patience and content-
ment by the promise of a future heaven. The
poor and the ignorant, the anarchistic and malignant, lift up their voice, and this voice is the roar
of the wild beast, crying out, " We demand a
portion of this world also." Now it is a vain
attempt to pacify the hunger of this fierce cry by
feeding out to it loaves of bread in the fashion of
ancient Rome, or bundles of secondhand clothing, or even the checks of rich men. These will
be received, but while they are being used the
givers will be cursed with curses deep and bitter.
There is no God in this form of beneficence, no
God for those who need Him most. There is not

the demonstration of disinterested love within it. No, the staff of indirection, of arm's-length service, of proxy virtue meets not, serves not, the great need of our day. The wild, restless, bitter unbelief of this day calls for personal contact— for the life and the hope which can be begotten in the hearts of the embittered and despairing by the breeding of personal interest and personal service—by that personal presence in earth's desolate field which shall illuminate the truth that the served and the servants are brothers, the children of a Father who is in heaven. The second requisition issues in the name of the lost faith which is humanity's supremest need.

A third requisition here issues in the name of the spiritual necessity of the giving life. Upon every side of us hundreds of human bodies are suffering from the lack of exercise. So hundreds of souls in the Christian communion are suffering from the lack of that personal effort which is the soul's best exercise. They hire the minister ; they hire the missionary ; they hire the charity agent ; they send a substitute for the Sunday-school, and so attempt to take all their spiritual exercise by proxy. The result of this is seen upon every side of us, in an uninterested and uninfluential Christian profession. How comparatively few of its members retain a lively concern in the affairs and the work of the church! How few of them are as strong in faith and as zealous of good works and as well-informed concerning the missionary work of the church as they were in the first years of their Christian life! One cause of this anæmia and lassitude, it cannot be doubted, is to be found in their attempt to take their spiritual exercise through the minister, through the missionary, through the agent, and through the check book. This proxy method empties the heart of its interest, and so leaves the life an easy prey for capture by the world. Now, personal work in the moral field would prevent all this. It would, first of all, widen the horizon of the individual life, so ennobling it. It is nothing less than a measureless pity that a woman who has been in discipleship to the Son of God for ten, twenty, forty years should to-day have nothing to talk about save her personal ailments and the trouble she has with her domestics. It is a great shame that a man who for one or two score years has been a confessed follower of Jesus Christ —of that Christ all of whose thoughts and words were world-wide—should to-day have his conversation and his interest bounded by his shop. Per-

2

sonal effort in the service of human need will prevent this narrowing and shallowing—this dwarfing of the human life. It will lead the individual up into an exceeding high mountain, from which he shall see that which is the only truly great entity of time, and, it may be, of the created universe, the flashing and the sweep and the roar of the great sea of humanity. It will introduce him to a brotherhood in the presence of whose pitiful need and tremendous interests the little ego shall cease from its tiny self-consciousness. It will widen the horizon of daily thought; inspire with nobler sympathies; dignify with higher purposes; and so insure the individual development of the worthier kind—prove the liberal education of the spirit. This is a University Extension course within the reach of the humblest human life. The third requisition issues in the name of individual need.

The fourth requisition issues in the name of the personal God and of the personal Jesus, God's manifestation in human form. The divine knowledge of all the creatures of His hand is individual. When the Creator looks over the heavens, the work of His hands, He does not say, " Behold a field of flying worlds "; rather these are His words: " Lift up your eyes on high, and behold who hath created these things, that bringeth out their host by number: he calleth them all by names . . . for that He is strong in power; not one faileth." And not otherwise is it in the field, the vast field, of human life. We speak of classes and masses. The divine knowledge makes use of no such raw and clumsy phrases. The Infinite Father knows the swarming millions of humanity as His individual children. He calls them by their name. He numbers the hairs of their heads. He has a bottle of remembrance for each one of their tears. He does not simply say, " Behold two sparrows !" but this rather,—one sparrow that shall fly and one that shall fall. God manifest in the flesh, behold how truly, how beautifully personal He was in all His relations with the human life—how He talked and blessed and saved by personal contact. The poor blind beggar's cry even He will not answer by proxy or indirection. Not to any one of his nearest attendants will He say, " Go and see what it is that that beggar wants." Nay, but He stops; He Himself responds to the pitiful cry; with His own voice He asks, " What wilt thou ?" Then listen to Him as He talks with Peter. How well He knows the eccentric disciple! How personal is His service of that disciple's need! Behold Him as He receives the head of the loving John upon His bosom. How true, how tender, His personal relations with this individual man!

Now, shall any one essay to honor or to continue this personal ministration of the Divine Lord through and by means of impersonal service, by the staff method? Will you hire a substitute and send this substitute to take your place by the side of such a Leader? Will you send a check as your only response, as your recognition of this example of personal service and personal love? Oh! if you do, it will be a shame unto you—a shame that shall one day flush your cheek with an intolerable burning. Oh, yes! hire a substitute for the day when the life of your fatherland hangs in the balance of the bloody battle; bid a servant answer the letter that has come from your lover; send a check unto the sorrow and loneliness of your mother; but do not think of putting off the Christ, who loved you and gave Himself for you, with any form of response that does not include your loyal, loving, personal service.

In the direction of this personal service lies, believe me, your finest earthly opportunity; your superior joy, and your richest reward. Oh, ye self-complacent men of bank, of office, and of store; ye children also of ease, of fashion, and of wealth, who vainly imagine that ye are dealing with the great things of this world, while ye turn over your Christ and your human brother to the substitute and to the machine, brush the scales from your eyes, unlearn your delusion before the sun of your earthly opportunity goes down in the night in which no man can work! Oh, ye helpers, ye teachers, ye missionaries, ye who are dealing with souls, and sometimes discouraged with a humility that disparages your work, this day also do ye repent of your unworthy shame and take unto your hearts the assurance that the mightiest issues of earth are those which ye are daily hand-ling—that the highest form of man's earthly life is that which is disclosed in the personal service of the needy human soul!

"And Gehazi came back to his master, saying, The child is not awaked. Master, the child is not awaked."

My fellow-men, the dead child before us is the heart's lost faith, the world's lost hope. And this machinery cannot give back. This the staff in the hand of a servant cannot quicken. This neither the written check nor the proxy hand can re-bestow. This lies dead until life is breathed into it by the living and loving spirit of the serving brother life.

My Christian friend, permit me to give you a personal introduction to your human brother who has need of you. Send him not your proxy, not the agent, not the check, but go yourself. So you will fill out the sweetest and the noblest obligation resting upon your earthly life. The love of your Father who is in heaven, and the need of your fellow-man who is on the earth—these two, through all the weary centuries of time, blend their deepest significance and their truest pathos in the words of this one voice : *We seek not yours, but you.*

II

THE DIVINE-HUMAN FACE

THE DIVINE-HUMAN FACE

" The glory of God in the face of Jesus Christ.'—2 COR. iv : 6.

GLORY is excellence in manifestation. The glory of the sun is in his out-streaming rays. The glory of nature is the beauty of the earth shown in mountain and valley, in lake and river, in forest and prairie. It is the gold of the flaming sunset; it is the silver gleam of the glancing river; it is the spotless ermine of the everlasting mountains.

So the glory of God is the divine excellence streaming forth in rays of moral splendor. The heavens declare the glory of God; and in the text it is declared that this glory shines in the face of Jesus Christ. Just as we might say the glory of day is in the face of the sun, the glory of night outrays from moon and star, so the Apostle, enlightened by the Divine Spirit, looks upon the face of Jesus of Nazareth and cries: " Behold the glory of God! Behold the manifestation of the Divine Excellence!"

The face of a man differs from every other part of the body in its superior power to express the life which is within the man. I say superior power, for every portion of the body possesses this attribute in a greater or less degree. Put the same garment successively on two different persons, and you will get widely different results. The form, the carriage, the characteristics of the body will strike through this covering. Leanness and fleshiness, grace and awkwardness, energy and languor, the stooping body and the erect form, will be clearly seen through the garments that shape themselves to the form which they enrobe. So human bodies disclose their individuality despite the art of costumer and tailor.

Now going a little deeper into these concentric layers that we call a human life, we come unto the body which the spirit wears for its vesture, even as the body wears the garments of which we have spoken; and no more than the outer does this inner conceal the life which it covers.

Look at the Frenchman's shoulders! His inner life bubbles up through them, even as the life of the boiling kettle bubbles up through the palpitating lid. Then there are the foot, the wrist, the neck, the contour and pose of the head, all of them voiceful of the inner life. Naturalists are able, from a single tibia, to construct the whole animal frame. Give them this one bone, and, upon it and round it, they will build up the body to which it belonged—to which it must have belonged. So might the anthropologist well-nigh construct the human mammal from the wrist bone or the cervical anatomy,—so instinct with individuality, so voiceful of the inner life, is every part of the human body.

But none of them is so much so as the face. When you would surely know whether a man is angry you do not look upon his back, or his hands, or his feet, but you look into his face. This is where the anger flashes out; this is the glass that is discolored by the vile breath of the soul; this is the shining disk over which moves the dark shadow of the eclipse; this is the limpid fountain that is muddied with passion's precipitate.

So also with joy. This too leaps from the heart into the face illuminating all its features. So also with sorrow. What a difference there is between the face of a sad, and the face of a joyous spirit! What two unlike pictures of a soul are given us in the faces of a crying and a laughing child! And states of the heart more permanent than the emotions find their expressions also in the face. Anxiety etches itself into the features; purity and impurity, benevolence and scorn, humility and pride, peace and unrest grow into engraver's lines upon its surface. So the face changes with the changes that go on within—now hardening, now softening, now laughing, now crying as the April day. If only we had the right kind of a microscope we might read in the face the whole history of the life—spelling out such words as these: success, failure, gentleness, scorn, sorrow, joy, peace, unrest, hope, fear—the very life of the soul. Hence, when we would begin the study of a man, if we have the opportunity, we always turn our eyes upon his face.

So let us at this time study the face that Jesus Christ turned upon this world, the face in which shone the glory of God. This let us do in order that we, coming to know what is the true glory of rational life, may be changed into the same image, even as by the Spirit of the Lord, or if not so much as this, yet at least that we may be made ashamed of some of the faces that we have turned upon the world, and which now, alas for us, are hung up in the gallery of the universe—in the rogue's gallery, some of them.

At the time in which Jesus lived, the publicans

were so many outcasts, political and social. In addition to being tax-collectors, they were the collectors of the taxes that the Roman Government had imposed. So they were doubly odious —odious because they were always raking in the money, and abominably odious because they collected this money for a foreign and a hated power; and being reckoned a degraded class, they became degraded. For it is hard, as Robertson has well said, for any man to live above the moral standard assigned to him by the community. The first step downward is to sink in the estimation of others; the next and fatal step is to sink in one's own estimation. The value of reputation is, that it pledges a man to be what he is taken for. It is indeed a fearful thing for a man to have no character to support—nothing to fall back upon in the hour of fierce assault, nothing to keep him up to himself in the day when the deadly simoom of temptation blows across his life.

Now the publicans had no character. They were outcasts from Jewish society, looked upon as vile and degraded by the community in which they lived. The religious classes, especially the Pharisees, particularly detested and avoided them. Well, one day after Jesus had begun His walks among men, it happened that His path led Him in the direction of one of these publicans who was sitting at the receipt of custom, engaged in his nefarious work of raking in the taxes.

The meeting is inevitable. Jesus and the pub-lican must see each other. What shall be the nature of this congress, what the result? With what glance will Jesus regard, what face will He turn upon the publican? The moment is a critical one, pent with an influence which shall tell upon all the ages, for the new man, the Lord from heaven, is walking toward the barrier set up by human society. What shall be the issue? Will He stop before reaching it—cowardly re-versing His course? Will He gently and deftly curve His pathway round it, as not many genera-tions ago some teachers of religion were accus-tomed to get round the slave pen and the human auction block? Or will He break through it? The moment is critical. Humanity's second Head, the new man from heaven, is walking toward the human life which this world has stamped "outcast." Will Jesus dare to recognize this life? Will He deign to interest Himself in it —to hope for it? With your own eyes and ears get the answer to these questions. For look! Jesus continues straight forward. Now He is even before the publican. See! He stops. He turns His face upon the publican. He speaks and the words that we hear are these: "Come, follow me"; and that same night Jesus accepts an invitation to dine at the publican's house.

Such was the meeting of the new Life of the new world with the outcast life of the old world. Such was the face that Jesus turned upon the man whom both society and the church had excommunicated. It was a face of sympathy and hope, of sympathy with and hope for a publican.

Such then, my fellow-men, is the glory of God. What, do you ask? Interest in a human life though the world treats it as refuse. To see manhood and divinity and hope in an outcast of earth. To lift up into companionship with Himself a social pariah—this is the glory of God, this is the outraying excellence of Deity, this is the outstreaming splendor of infinite Being, for this is that which shone in the face that Jesus turned that day upon the man who was a publican.

Take another incident—look upon another of the faces which Jesus turned upon this world. One day, during the press of His public duties, among those who sought the presence of Jesus were a number of parents who brought their children with them, that the Saviour might place His hands, in blessing, upon the heads of the little ones.   The disciples of the Lord, imagining themselves to have their Master in charge, and not willing that His time should be taken up with such petty cares, rebuked the solicitous parents. " For shame," they cried, " do you not see that the Master's time is all required for duties of the largest and most important character?   How then can you be so thoughtless as thus to intrude upon Him?   Would you have Jesus waste His time upon children ? "

Jesus, listening, hears these words of His disciples, and at once breaks in upon them with this voice: "Suffer the little children to come unto me, and forbid them not."   Then turning to the little ones, and reaching forth His arms He cries, "Come," and as they run unto Him, He takes them up in His arms, puts His hands upon them and blesses them.

My hearers, the picture is not dim unto this day nor is its central figure indistinct.   Across the field of nineteen centuries, see it—Jesus holding a little child in His arms.   Some of us have known hours when, with tear-filled eyes, we could see nothing else save this picture—the Saviour lifting up the little one from our arms unto His.   Again, to-day, I would have you look upon it—for it is beautiful.

Behold that face which Jesus turns upon the child within His arms! See you the light that is in it? That is the glory of God in the face of Jesus Christ.

Let me ask you, Who is your God? What is He? The Being whose glory fills the heavens above, whose majestic splendor is reflected from those myriad suns, which along the paths of the infinite field lead forth their glorious train? Think you of Him only as the mighty One, who upon that far distant and shadowy throne executes the purpose of an infinite will—electing unto life, reprobating unto death, stretching out over immensity the scepter of an unchangeable and omnipotent decree? The glory of God in your eyes, is it only the resplendent shining of that august and sovereign throne? Or a thousandfold worse is this phrase—the glory of God—only an empty form of words, with which you have been accustomed to round out the sentence in the stereotyped prayer? Ah! I bid you see this glory made real before your eyes, brought near unto human vision, made plain and simple unto human intelligence. The light in Jesus' face as He looks upon the little child in His arms—that is the glory of God, and neither Orion nor the Pleiades shows forth this glory better.

Cast your eyes over the world. Wherever you see a human face beaming in gentleness and love upon a little child—there is the glory of God before your very eyes. Wherever you see a human face scowling upon the child life, though this face belongs to one who has been years here praying that he might live to the glory of God, be sure that this prayer has been of words only and that it is yet unheard in the realms above.

But pass to another incident, to look upon another face which Jesus turned upon this world in which we live.

A certain Pharisee besought the Saviour to dine with him, and Jesus went in and sat down to meat. And when the Pharisee saw it he marveled that Jesus had not first washed before dinner. And this was the face that Jesus turned upon him: "Woe unto you, Pharisees! for ye tithe mint and rue and all manner of herbs, and pass over judgment and the love of God." "Woe unto you, scribes and Pharisees, hypocrites! for ye make clean the outside of the cup and of the platter, but within they are full of extortion and excess. . . . Ye serpents, ye generation of vipers, how can ye escape the damnation of hell?"

Such was the terrible face that Jesus turned upon Phariseeism; and this is still before the world and for our observation and study to-day.

The best that can be said of the God who is set forth by many religious teachers of our day is that He is a goodish old Father who loves all the children of men. He would, it is true, prefer that these children should obey Him; but, if not, He will make all necessary allowances, putting up with whatever of recognition and loyalty they are willing to bestow upon Him. Now, concerning this sentimental Deity, this must be said first of all. He is despicable even in the eyes of those who have made Him. The Jove of the mythical world was the thunderer; his hands were filled with flaming bolts. He stood for strength, for power, for grandeur of being. His name was coherence for his mighty realm, and the roll of his chariot wheels was the glory of his kingdom. Mythology at least made its god respectable in the eyes of his subjects. But the dilettantism of some modern pulpits paints the great Jehovah as an enthroned emotion, a doting old Father, a King—if He can be called a King—who if placed upon an earthly throne would nauseate His realm and vex it with innumerable ills.

I tell you, my fellow-men, this old and wicked

world, these vast cities upon its surface, raging with iniquity and as impure as hell, demand a God of justice and of strength, an actual ruler to sit upon the throne of the heavens. Every virtuous mind, too, craves such a God. Judgment and justice, let these be the habitation of His throne; terrible things in righteousness, let these be the thunders of His mighty realm. So prays every pure and noble spirit.

Again, it must be said of this God of the modern amenities that He is not the One whose glory shines in the face upon which we have just looked. "Ye serpents, ye generation of vipers, how can ye escape the damnation of hell?" It is the glory of the true God, that when there is need He can shoot such thunderbolts as these. Against Phariseeism and hypocrisy, and all falsehood, all sham and cant, and lying formality, the glory of God (oh! let the earth give thanks) shows as a consuming fire. This face of Jesus Christ, I beseech you, look well upon it. Its indignation leaps forth as the lightning from the livid cloud! Its words are the thunders of eternal righteousness, reverberating over the head of defiant and shameless sin! All this that you see and feel —all this splendor of terribleness—is the glory of God raying forth upon the world, the glory of God focused in a human face.

Yet once again I would have you look upon the face of Jesus as it is turned upon our world. A poor guilty woman—guilty as only woman can be—lies crouching in the dust at the Saviour's feet. Friend she has none; hope she has none. The angry crowd surges up to the prostrate form, panting, ravenous for blood. Jesus is silent. We cannot even see His face this moment, for it is bent upon the ground upon which He is writing with His finger. It is the face of the new man, the Lord from heaven—what is in it? It is a face which shall never fade from earth's vision—what is in it? It is the face in which shines the glory of God—what shall we see in it when it is raised? Indifference? Disgust? Contempt? Anger? Wait a moment! There now, Jesus moves; He lifts his head. Oh, see that face! How different from any face in the impatient and ravening crowd! How different from any face which the world had ever seen before! What tenderness is in it! What love! What serene calmness! What courage for pity and forgiveness! Then, while we look, this face melts into speech, and these are its words, " Neither do I condemn thee: go, and sin no more." This

the glory of God? Why, then, those holy
Pharisees had not known God! This the glory
of God? Why, then, there are self-styled wor-
shipers of God upon every side of us who do
not know Him. This the glory of God? Then
what must be said of many circles of earth's good
society? Why, that their glory is the glory, not
of God, but of devils!

But look once more, and upon another face
which Jesus turned upon our world. For long
hours now He has been exposed to taunt and
ridicule. He has been buffeted, smitten in the
face, spit upon, and crowned in mockery with
thorns. And now the culmination has come.
Wicked hands have lifted Him to the Cross and
nailed Him there, and, their horrid task accom-
plished, His executioners now sit down at the foot
of the Cross to divide His raiment among them.
It is at this juncture that Jesus turns His eyes
upon them. Behold this face, and scan it well!
for here again you shall behold the glory of God.
Remember, it is a face which out of its own mortal
agony looks down upon His executioners. What
is in the face? Revenge? Wrath? Flaming
indignation? Let it speak its own meaning;
" Father, forgive them; for they know not what
they do."

The mad tragedy reels onward. Jesus has now been for hours upon the Cross. The derisive shout no longer falls upon His ears. The angry crowd is tired, satiated. Jesus is dying; Jesus is dying. But, as we stand waiting for the end, a piteous entreaty falls upon our ears. It comes not from the throng before the Cross, but from one of the three crosses. It is from a dying thief, who but a short time since had joined in the general reviling. Listen to his pitiful words : " Lord, remember me when Thou comest into Thy kingdom." Jesus turns His eyes, rays of the divine glory stream through His face and fall upon the dying malefactor in this response : " To day shalt thou be with Me in Paradise."

What is the lesson from it all ? Interest in man as man apart from and independent of all external circumstances—this is the glory of God. Interest in and love for little children—this is the glory of God. Burning wrath flaming out against all hypocrisy—this is the glory of God. Pity and forgiveness for the vilest outcast who will go and sin no more—this is the glory of God. Mercy and pardon ready to flow unto a dying criminal— this is the glory of God. Look well, I pray you, upon the faces; live with them looking down upon you—read the glory and learn your God.

Only two or three brief inferences :—

First, the glory of God as it shines in the face of Jesus Christ is excellence that approves itself unto the human consciousness and which lies in the path of human development. We are made in the divine image, and there is not a face that Jesus turned upon the world but we can easily conceive of as belonging to a perfect man. Oh, yes, it is true! He is the model man, He is the perfect man, He is the divine man, and He leads in the direction of all true and beautiful development. Type and prophecy is He of the new race which, in the regeneration, shall enter into everlasting possession of the new earth. Aye! the day cometh—in God's Book it is written—when every human face in the beautiful second order shall shine with the glory that beamed from the face of earth's Redeemer.

Second, the glory of God which many a theological system and many a religious confession exalts is only a caricature of the true glory. Men have shut themselves up in monastic cells for the glory of God. They have endured bodily torture ; they have drunk the blood of heretics ; they have reprobated earth's great majority, and they themselves have professed a willingness to be damned—and all for the glory of God! And now? Why proud faces, selfish and hard faces, faces which are frowns at home and flints in the world; men who place money above conscience, and women who would rather be society's elect than heaven's—these all profess communion with the Christ, and imagine they are showing forth the glory of God!

Again, that shining face that we have looked upon to-day is the goal which the Christian ought to keep continually in view. By it he should test his hope, and by it he should measure his progress. We deal too much in abstractions. We talk too much of a plan of salvation. We lay too much stress upon one particular heart emotion or mental activity that we denominate faith, and which on the principle of a *quid pro quo* is in some mysterious way to avail for our future welfare. Some Christians lift Jesus up out of His own gospel—leaving only a "plan of salvation" behind. Some Christians lift up character out of religion, leaving only churchmanship in its place. My fellow-men, I warn you back this day to the concrete. The only plan of salvation is the loving, living Saviour, who is Jesus the Christ; and the only evidence that we have part or lot in His salvation is found in our growing likeness to Him.

Therefore, I say, keep the face of Jesus daily and distinctly before you. Let it be the ever-shining goal of your hope and your endeavor. But see to it that it is the face of the Jesus of the Bible. Theology has pictured this face, but you do not want her engraving — cold and hard. Sentimentality has painted the face, but you do not want her daub. What you need as your inspiration, as your beacon light, as your shining goal, is the original of the Bible gallery—the face which was turned in sympathy and hope upon the outcast publican; which beamed with love upon little children; which beat down in blazing wrath upon Phariseeism; which looked love and spoke forgiveness unto the dying thief—the original face—this hang up before your life for its daily rebuke and measureless inspiration.

But say you, " My heart is without admiration for that face!" Then woe are you in the universe of God, for that face stands for divine beauty, is the outraying of that character which alone is blessed while eternity lasts. But say you: " It is so far above me, I can never reach unto it; the hard lines of my face I can never smooth and round into those beautiful features." Ah! I know it. But a power is at hand to supplement your weakness—the power of a divine regeneration.

"For we all, with unveiled face, beholding as in a mirror the glory of the Lord, are transformed into the same image, from glory to glory, even as from the Lord the Spirit."

Let us then study the face of Jesus Christ, finding the correction of our errors of head, finding also all needed inspiration for the heart, in the daily and diligent contemplation of that human face in which shines the true glory of rational being—through which God looks out upon us and upon our world.

Now, I beg you, wait just a moment. Before you go I desire to hang up these several faces of Jesus in the room of your soul. The face looking upon the degraded and outcast publican I will hang yonder in the vestibule at the very entrance. The face of Jesus looking upon the little child which He holds in His arms I will hang there above the mantel. The face of Jesus turned upon Phariseeism I will hang opposite the window yonder, in the strongest light of all. The face of Jesus looking upon the woman who was a sinner shall go in yonder quiet niche, that the one who desires to study it may turn aside and be alone. The face that Jesus from the cross turned upon His executioners—this would better rest upon the easel, inviting daily and closest examination.

Now there is but one face left—the face with which Jesus answered the prayer of the dying criminal. Carry this, I pray you, in miniature locket over your heart, for it is in strongest focus, not only the glory, but the glory of the glory of that God whose name is Love, and whose love is the beautiful Hope of your soul.

III

THE SKEPTICISM OF PROMINENT PEOPLE

III

THE SKEPTICISM OF PROMINENT PEOPLE

"Whosoever shall not receive the kingdom of God as a little child shall in no wise enter therein."—LUKE xviii : 17.

YET I think we are in danger of laying especial emphasis upon their relation to religion, of a mind and spirit in character the opposite, and in position the antipodes of the child mind and the child spirit. I refer to the importance which is so generally attributed to the unbelief or skepticism of persons prominent in the world, prominent in letters, or science, or business, or society, or politics. Now far be it from me to say that the believing soul can remain altogether insensible to the assaulting force of skepticism. I will not even deny that there is much truth in honest doubt, or that from this doubt there has not broken forth much light for the service of the world. All that I desire at this time to say unto you, at the bidding of the text and for the reassurance and comfort of your faith, is this: We are in danger of attaching too much importance unto, and of laying too strong an emphasis upon, the unbelief and irreligion of the world's prominent people.

I. Consider, first, that large knowledge in one direction often exists with notorious ignorance upon other subjects and along other lines of thought. Yonder university has subdivided the field of human knowledge into many sections, assigning a specialist to each. Generally speaking, in his own particular branch too, the professor is somewhat of an authority. He is not much, however, outside his own specialty. On a question of Christian casuistry the opinion of the mathematician has no especial value. This is because he has not given attention to such matters; because he is not learned in this direction. On a vexed question in the field of biology the astronomer, however eminent, would not be taken as authority. This is because he has not made biology a study, because he has given little or no attention to its mighty theories.

Humbler illustrations of this principle lie all about us. There, side by side, are the offices of lawyer and doctor. Both of these are now called to the bedside of the dying man—the one to make his will, the other to prescribe for his suffering body. Suppose, now, that these two men, through some mistake, were made to change places—the doctor being called on to construct the legal paper and the lawyer to write out the Latin prescription. Do you not see how ignorant and how helpless the men would be, and this no matter how proficient each of them may be in his own calling? This is because the men are out of their spheres. The doctor can easily and confidently guide unto the condition where wills must be made. That is his business. The lawyer can take the man from the hand of the physician (not his affair to know how he came there) and iron-clad his pleasure concerning the estate which he is to leave behind him.

So it is through all the industrial and professional callings. Human strength is weakness; human skill is ignorance outside of the narrow range of a very small circle.

In a wider view, the same truth appears. Phidias was a wonderful sculptor. He could make marble speak, but he himself could never have spoken the Oration on the Crown. It required a Demosthenes to do this. Raphael is a master for all time in painting, but Raphael could not sing what Dante sang. Mozart and Mendelssohn—we bow to them in music, but we accept not their *dicta* in political economy, or architecture, or law. In these matters the opinions of Adam Smith, and Christopher Wren, and Blackstone are a thousandfold more valuable.

This principle brought thus clearly into view is sadly transgressed when men of literature, or science, or public life open their mouths to speak upon the laws and verities of the spiritual kingdom. Learned in other directions, they may be, and often are, but as often are they ignorant of religion and of all that pertains to it, and their criticisms and conclusions are of no particular value.

Suppose that the professor has literally and for all his life peered through the microscope; that he is an authority, and the highest one, in this important subdivision of the kingdom of knowledge. But what qualification is this for a critic or a prophet in the spiritual realm? None whatever. The famous microscopist makes a fool of himself if he opens his mouth authoritatively on spiritual matters. The spirit, whether divine or human, the Christ, the spores of moral evil, the movements of the conscience and the will—these never come into view under the eye of the microscope, however much its power may be magnified. The same may be said with reference to all these attainments of the human mind that go under the name of scientific. Spirit cannot be resolved, cannot be analyzed in the crucible of the chemist. The human soul cannot be placed in a glass jar and its operations watched, as the cocoon is scrutinized and the law of the butterfly laid down. The laws of moral influence and moral inspiration cannot be figured out and formulated as are the orbits of the planets. So it is very possible for a man to be learned in the movements of the heavenly bodies and yet blind to the radiant footsteps of their Creator. A professor may know much of light and heat and motion, and yet be utterly ignorant of the laws of spiritual influence. A man may be able to construct a profound essay, to sing a beautiful poem; but these, his power and performance, qualify him not at all to speak with any especial significance upon the subjects of inspiration and prayer and faith. We do learning or culture entirely too much honor when we grant to them any especial authority within the spiritual realm. The simple truth is this: it matters little what a mathematician, or a chemist, or a biologist, or a *littérateur*, as such, may think or may say of God and of Christ, of sin and of immortality. To use a homely phrase—these things are not in their line. To them they have given no especial attention,

and upon them they have no right to speak dic-
tatorially.

With a question of health I will not go to the
lawyer; with a question of conscience I will not
go to the politician; with a question of taste I
will not go to the rich parvenu; and with a question about God, or Christ, or my soul, I will not go
to the man who is color-blind to the light which
shines in the face of Jesus Christ, and who has
never lifted a prayer to the God of heaven. Wise
he may be in some things, learned along certain
lines where I am ignorant, but ignorant also is he
upon larger and grander subjects, concerning
which I am sure that I know something.

II. But again and in this same connection I
consider a second general fact, viz., that the constituent entities of religion lie quite outside the
sphere of human discovery and so cannot be
reached by the process of human reason.

The truth here I can lift up before you in the
form of a picture. No doubt the astronomer,
through the telescope of yonder observatory, can
see farther into the heavens than can you with
the unassisted eye. But suppose the problem is
to discover and tabulate the flora of Sirius. Now
which is better, your eye or the astronomer's lens?
Why, both are equally worthless. You must ex-

claim, " My eyes cannot reach unto such objects through such a distance." And the astronomer must reply, " The telescope was not made to discover lichens upon the surface of a world so far removed." But even this is not a sufficiently strong representation of the case. Imagination can conceive of a telescope of such wondrous power as even to fasten upon these humble growths upon the rocks of the distant star. But deity, but spirit, but heaven—all the objects of the spiritual world—are not so related to the possibility of vision. Let therefore the illustration be changed. Be the problem to discover a spirit upon the far distant shores of the mighty sun. Now let the astronomer raise his telescope to the skies, and you, your unhelped eyes. Can he see farther than you ? But what of this ? Farther ! what does this signify when infinity still lies beyond ? Farther ! what an idle world when the invisible is to be discovered !

Do you not see that as to the end proposed you and the astronomer are on a level ? And let human learning stand for the telescope, and our illustration is transposed into the key of the text. In many directions it is granted that the great man will see farther than you. Into matter and its laws, into heat and light and motion, into the

strata that make up the crust of the earth, into
the fauna and flora that are distributed upon its
surface—in all these directions the vision of the
learned man will outstrip yours. But let the
problem be the discovery, the vision of God, of
spirit, of the post-mortem state, and what shall
the philosopher do above and beyond you? Is
he not, with all his learning, on a level with you
and your ignorance? Most surely he is. And
there is ever so good an explanation of his limitation. Learning counts for nothing, science
counts for nothing here, because their methods
and processes cannot be transferred to the spiritual realm. *Induction is an absurdity where
observation is an impossibility.* And this is the
case in the moral world. "God is the one whom
no man hath seen nor can see." Why, then, shall
we allow ourselves to be troubled by the skepticism of human learning? It has seen nothing of God which we have not seen. Nay, more.
It cannot come unto the sight of anything in the
spiritual realm, the vision of which is forbidden
to us.

All the things which are sought here are known
only as they are revealed to the spirit of a man.
And have we not spirits? Can we not go unto
the Great Spirit? Must we forsooth have mastered

a few theories as to the origin and laws of matter? Must we know a few facts about light and heat and electricity in order that we may be favorably introduced to the Father of our souls, in order that we may be qualified to receive spiritual impressions, to respond to the great influence of the moral world?

The supposition is absurd. As well say that we must know Greek, or have made a million of dollars, before God will hear us, or before we can read His word. I tell you, my fellow-Christians, the truth is self-evident. With reference to the knowledge that buttresses the religious life, we are on a level with the most prominent and the most cultured. Revelation is an absolute necessity to us both. Without this the greatest man is left in ignorance, and with it we know easily as much as he.

III. But still farther, and in the same direction, I must ask you to consider that the habits of intellectual culture often have a strong tendency to disqualify for the attainment of spiritual knowledge.

Every department of human knowledge has its own proper and necessary condition. In the sphere of the artist this condition is the love of the beautiful, the inborn sense and faculty of taste.

A mathematician might gaze on the landscape as long and as faithfully as the artist, but he would not see its beauty. This would be hidden from him, because he has not conformed to the condition upon which this beauty is revealed. This law runs, too, through all the knowledges. The poet can never enter into the kingdom of the fixed sciences. He is disqualified by his mental habits and by the very nature of his being. The empirical student can see no beauty in the sweetly singing lines of poetry. He would need to be reborn in order to hear and feel this melody.

Now in keeping with this general law and under its sway is the spiritual kingdom. The reception of its truth also calls for, demands, a certain prerequisite in the life of the learner. This is laid down by the highest authority in such words as these :—

" The secret of the Lord is with them that fear Him."

" To this man will I look, even to him that is of a poor and of a contrite spirit."

" If any man will do His will, he shall know of the doctrine."

" Blessed are the pure in heart: for they shall see God."

We see thus what is the condition that obtains

and governs in the sphere of religious truth.   It
is, as we would expect to find it—a moral one.
The dictum is: Bring to the study of spiritual
things a pure heart and an obedient life, and you
shall have good success.   But this condition the
man of science often neglects, ignores.   He will
take into the spiritual realm the methods and processes of science.   Instead of a pure and loving
heart, he brings the faculty of trained observation;
instead of the obedient life, he comes for the con-
quest armed with a keen and vigorous intellect.
All knowledge he cries is induction from observation.   Let me see, let me reason, let me demonstrate; and with this contemptuous disregard
of spiritual method he goes to work.   He, forsooth, will discover immortality in the structure
of the body—in the seat of a gland, in the con-
volution of a nerve, in the arrangement of the
bioplastic atoms.

Of course, his end is failure.   God is not so
found; nor spirit, nor immortality so demonstrated.
But most justly, the failure here, and any unbelief arising from it, may be set down as the
result of an unauthorized and a vicious method.
The man has stalked rudely and coarsely into the
spiritual world, as rudely and coarsely as if with
blare of trumpet, and helmeted head, and leveled

spear he should break into nature's beautiful works, to conquer landscape effects—so to woo the goddess of beauty!

Professing himself to be wise he has become a fool. So it was in Corinth and at Athens of old. Paul's preaching was to them foolishness, because it could not be run into the syllogism or into the philosophy of the schools. But their boasted wisdom is cast-off rubbish to-day, while Paul's foolishness seems good for generations yet to come.

But without further dwelling upon this point, let me stop to ask, "When is the necessity of attaching any especial emphasis to the unbelief of human learning?" It does not adhere to the spiritual method. The fundamental condition of spiritual certitude it ignores. Much learning has brought upon it, if not madness, yet a manner quite repellent to all spiritual verity. Be so wise then as to save your fear for another and an entirely different case.

Wait till there comes to you a pure and reverent spirit—I care not how humble or unlearned—that can say, "I have loved, I have obeyed, I have prayed, I have laid my heart open in the simplicity of a little child—and still your God, your Christ, your immortal hope are as myths and fables to my soul."

Before such a case as this, when it shall appear, let your faith fear and betake itself to a reëxamination of its defenses. But before the man who has studied in a newspaper office and graduated from a clubroom; before the Ishmaelite who parades the country over, for five hundred dollars a night, caricaturing all great and sacred things; before the politician whose success has come through the debasement of his better self and nobler being; before the professor of physics who has not discovered the eternal Spirit as he might a new line in the solar spectrum—before such as these, possess your soul in patience and your faith in confidence. Spiritual truth and spiritual hopes have never promised themselves unto such seekers. Such have, such get, what they desire. They have their reward, but this reward is not any one of the things that God has prepared for them that love Him. To every knowledge is its own fixed condition. You cannot see the odor of a rose. You cannot weigh the glories of a sunset in a grocer's scale. You cannot analyze the beauty of a lily or violet. You cannot mathematically demonstrate the winsomeness and the worthiness of virtue. So the things of God are not the product

of human cerebration, but are His revelation unto
the humble and reverent spirit of His human
child.

IV. But I must add yet again that we ought
not to allow ourselves to be greatly troubled by
the skepticism of prominent people, for the reason
that this unbelief may be punitive in its nature—
the penalty of a false and bad life.

In many parts of the Bible it is written down in
plainest words that light is withdrawn from those
who will not walk in it; that the cataract of
unbelief gathers over the eyes which will not
look upon truth when she stands radiant before
them. Listen to these words from the lips of
Jesus: "Walk while ye have the light, that darkness overtake you not. . . While ye have the
light, believe on the light, that ye may become
sons of light;" and these other ominous words:
" Because they received not the love of the truth
. . . God shall send them strong delusion, that
they should believe a lie."

We have no reason to conclude that this law
is inoperative in our day. Inoperative? Why,
have we not with our own eyes seen cultured and
learned men turn away from the great, broad
teachings of Jesus Christ unto table tippings and
the materialization of spirits? Have we not seen

men, wearing the laurels of science on their brows, close their eyes to the glory of a personal Creator and turn unto matter as holding within it the promise and potency of every form of life? Do we not in this present day have before our eyes the spectacle of men prominent in the world of law and letters, in pitiful bondage to a coarsely-shrewd, and grotesquely-pretentious woman?

What is the explanation of all this—this of great men showing themselves so little, this of the unbeliever having become so credulous as to hug to his bosom the most puerile nonsense? Read the explanation in the great law of the moral world to which I have referred.

What then shall we do? What shall be our attitude toward such skepticism? Shall we refuse to look upon the sun, because there are those who have chosen darkness rather than light and lost their sight by so doing? Because moral law has visited its penalty of the darkened under-standing upon those who walked not in the light when it was given them, shall we therefore turn from the same light?

Rather is there not just here a measureless admonition that we should cleave unto the truth which we know, and hasten to embody it in our lives? Carlyle, in speaking upon the law and the penalty here, quotes from the Koran this incident of certain dwellers by the Dead Sea to whom Moses was sent: "They sniffed and sneered at the prophet, saw no comeliness in him, and so he withdrew. But nature and other rigorous voracities did not withdraw. When next we find these dwellers by the Dead Sea they are, according to the Koran, all changed into apes. By not using their souls they lost them, and now their only employment is to sit there and look out into the dreariest and most undecipherable sort of a universe. Only once in seven days do they remember that they once had souls." And to this incident the stern prophet of reality appends these quaint and penetrating words: " Have you never, my reader, in your travels fallen in with parties of the tribe? Methinks they have grown quite numerous of late."

Oh, yes, numerous surely! The foolish wise man, the believing unbeliever, credulous of the flimsiest speculations and the crudest guesses, swallowing readily the baldest contradictions of soul-consciousness and spiritual intuition, willing to take up with any " ism," no matter how absurd —he is upon every side of us.

But wherever he appears, he is the embodied penalty of moral law: one who has lost his soul by not using it : a living illustration of the great truth that light cannot be scorned with impunity : a moving statue of one who professing himself to be wise has become a fool, and who is now compelled to and fro throughout the earth, that with garrulous lips he may warn the truth-respecting and the self-respecting soul from his own pitiful doom.

My fellow-Christians, it is the characteristic of every age and of individual life to imagine that its experience is peculiar. So strong and general is this tendency, that an inspired apostle deemed its correction nothing less than a comfort and an inspiration. "Think it not strange," writes he, "concerning the fiery trial which is to try you as though some strange thing happened unto you." And again he writes, "There hath no temptation taken you but such as is common to man." And so I say unto you to-day, you who are fighting the good fight of faith, no strange thing has happened unto you. You may be saying within yourself, "Science is arraying itself against religion; everywhere the banner of infidelity is being lifted up—there never was such a day." But in this you are mistaken. Listen to this voice from out St. Peter's day : "Where is the promise of His coming? for since the fathers fell asleep, all things continue as they were from the beginning of the creation." That is, the natural, that which we can see, is all that we can know of. So agnosticism is at least eighteen centuries old. Listen again as Paul gives voice to a special danger of his day: "They teach things which they ought not, for filthy lucre's sake." There is your infidel lecturer, your skeptical professor in the first century. And again the same apostle writes to Timothy: "Keep that which is committed to thy trust, avoiding profane and vain babblings, and oppositions of science falsely so called." There is scientific skepticism nineteen hundred years deep in the past.

I tell you that every generation of Christians, since the Cross ran red upon Calvary, has held to faith against the same assaults that you feel and fear to-day. If you cannot triumph over these assaults, if you cannot hold on to faith against these oppositions, then are you no true descendants of those who have entered into rest, and now hang above you as a great cloud of witnesses.

And I beseech you, if your faith is growing weak, if you feel that it is trembling before the assaults of skepticism, seek not to bolster it up by counter arguments. Turn rather from the unworthiness in your life. Repent of your dis-

loyalty to truth already known. Seek the true;
love the pure; do the good.   Live nearer to Him
who is the truth.   Open your heart to the inflow-
ing of the divine Spirit. Show all reverence to
your spiritual intuitions.   Plead the promise, " If
any man lack wisdom, let him ask of God, and it
shall be given him."

So shall the great things of the spiritual world
daily become more certain to your soul; so shall
profane and vain babblings cease to trouble you;
so shall the scraps of human learning fall upon
your great certitude and cause not a tremor within
it; and so with peace in the heart, along the path
that shines brighter and brighter, shall you pass
forward until the veil drops from your eyes and
you stand face to face with the solved mystery of
the universe.   Do not imagine that the condition
here is some wonderful spiritual elevation.   The
water-drop reflects the glorious sun, and so a
thought of tender love, so an act of gentle kindness may reveal the Infinite Goodness, and make
the whole spiritual universe real unto your soul.

Ye who would come unto a stronger faith, remember that the sublime verities of the moral
world are hidden from the "wise and prudent."
Remember that a man may be over-smart, over-
wise toward God—so wise and so smart that

loving Omniscience must abandon the hope of teaching him.   Remember also that childhood is nearest to truth, and love, and God, and that into the kingdom of heaven, easily and forevermore, enters the one who becomes as a little child.

IV

JESUS' ROYAL GRANT TO THE HUMAN HEART

IV

JESUS' ROYAL GRANT TO THE HUMAN HEART

"Be not therefore anxious for the morrow."—MATT. vi : 34.

AT the very outset, and with all confidence, we may say that the Saviour does not issue this injunction against prevision, against the anticipation of the future by which man seems to be distinguished from the brutes that perish. Faith, which is fundamental in religion, is the substance of things hoped for, the evidence of things not seen. "By faith, Noah being warned of God of things not seen as yet, prepared an ark." "By faith, Abraham when he was called to go out into a place which he should afterwards receive for an inheritance, obeyed; and he went out not knowing whither he went." One of the most characteristic and general confessions of the Christian centuries has its expression in these words, "We walk by faith, not by sight." Jesus' own admonitions, and exhortations, and teachings, even the solemnest of them, reach out unto and take hold of the future, finding in this future both their

justification and their emphasis. Yes, surely religion is a dealing in moral futures! And we cannot believe that the great Teacher, with one voice
fixes our attention upon the future, and with
another voice bids us forget that future. He does
not with one hand burn the morrow into our souls,
and with the other shut it out from our thoughts.
No! the injunction of the text is not against prevision, not against the anticipation of the future,
but against anxiety, against gnawing, weakening,
distressing care.

This injunction also is issued only to a certain
kind or type of human life.

Will you go to the man who is giving way to
the passion for strong drink and say, " Be not
anxious for the morrow "? To the man who is
living beyond his means and embezzling money
to keep up the vicious and pitiful display, will you
go and say, " Be not anxious for the morrow "?
Why, both of these classes and all their kindred
ought to be full of anxiety for the future. So not
to the human life which is forgetting God and
restraining prayer and neglecting duty; not to
the one who is living the mere sense life, as if
there was no such thing as responsibility, or sin,
or judgment, or God, not to such a type of life
does Jesus ever say, " Be not anxious for the

future"; but to the reverent, the thoughtful, the conscientious, to the man who is doing the best he knows, to the life which is purposely and lovingly a child of the Great Father—to this one the voice of Jesus comes evermore in the shape of these beautiful words, " Be not anxious for the morrow."

But how shall we come to heed this injunction of our Lord ? How shall we come to face, and to make continual approach to the type of life that its words disclose and authorize ? What is the basis, standing upon which, we may intelligently and hopefully strive to come unto faith of soul, calmness of life, and trust for the future ? Some exclusions must be made here, and those without hesitation.

First, will-power. It is vain to say, " I will not worry." This for two reasons. The will has no such power over the heart, and this power, whatever its strength to-day, may itself be undermined and fall into a pitiful weakness. Neither can we successfully address ourselves to the life-lesson set before us by the Saviour under the direction of youth and health. The strength of to-day may vanish in the sickness of to-morrow, and youth is an unreliable confidence, an ally whose forces are continually deserting us. Neither can earthly abundance help us greatly here. 'Money cannot feed the heart with peace even when it is with us, and we know that it cannot go with us into many of the morrows which shall be most prolific of anxiety. What power shall money have to serve us in the morrow of sorrow? in the morrow of pain? in the morrow of world-leaving? in the morrow of judgment?

If then these exclusions and all similar ones must be unhesitatingly made, what is left us as preparation for obedience to the injunction of the Saviour?

Simply this: We must have in full and forceful heart-possession the conviction which warrants the banishment of anxiety. This is made up of two parts—the one, a fact which we all do know and which Jesus lifted up into unfading light, and the other the truth which He came into the world to reveal and to teach. This fact is the impotency of man; this truth is the love of God. Our hope then, and our only hope, of coming unto the life, the blessed life unto which Jesus calls, lies in our realization of these two great laws:

First, the helplessness of man over the morrow. Secondly, the love of God that embosoms this morrow.

Now let me serve you as best I may in this

hour, by echoing within your ears and hearts the voices with which Jesus teaches these two great conditions of the trustful and happy life.

Listen, first of all, to His voice as He sets forth the pitiful impotency of man:

"Which of you by taking thought can add one cubit unto his stature?" "If ye then be not able to do that thing which is least, why take ye thought for the rest?" Dwell, I pray you, for a moment upon this declaration, if so be it may sink into your heart with its blessed power of emancipation and of trust.

The helplessness of the human life in relation to the future is so complete as to be fairly pitiful. It reaches even unto the extent of absolute ignorance of this future. "For ye know not what shall be on the morrow." How then can you prepare for the unseen? How can your anxiety set in order that which is and must remain absolutely unknown? The curtain may rise upon a scene of joy or upon a scene of sorrow: upon health or upon sickness: upon the bountiful fruition of your dearest hopes or upon these hopes withered and scattered as so many autumn leaves. It may rise upon a scene in which success shall sit at her ease while the golden horn of plenty empties itself into her overflowing lap, or it may rise upon a scene of poverty, bare and bleak, swept by biting winds and overhung with wrathful clouds. What now? Shall your soul consume itself with anxiety over the to-morrow which may come to mock all your anticipations? Shall you prepare for adversity, when in the book of the future, prosperity is written over against your name? Shall you arrange a bottle for your tears, when God intends that you shall laugh instead? Oh, how many human lives have prepared for a future which they never were to see; arranged for the crossing of bridges unto which they never were to come; laboriously planned for the rolling away of stones, which they were to find, when they came up to them, already rolled away! How many have anticipated with anxiety the days and the cares of old age when it was written in God's book that they should die young! How many have fretted their souls over coming poverty, and with fingers of borrowed care have raveled out the beautiful garment of present happiness, when heaven's voice had said of the future, Let it bring them riches! What a countless number of parents have worried themselves over the future settlement of their children, have fed their souls with increasing anxiety as to what their children would do when bereft of parental love and care, when it was God's purpose all the while to take the children first! What numbers throughout the world have looked forward to and laid their plans for the quiet evening of life when business should be laid aside and all its rasping cares dismissed, and then have dropped dead in the harness, its galls and abrasions so many running sores upon all their being!

It is surely one of the most solemn and pathetic thoughts which can enter the mind of man that a very large if not the greater part of the suffering of human hearts has been over things that never were to be—has been trouble borrowed in view of imaginary days and imaginary dangers. I can see him now—the rich fool as he starts forth from the canvas of the Great Master. He is in great perplexity of mind over what he shall do with his ripening fruits and increasing goods. Even his present abundance he could not enjoy, so full was he of anxiety over the new barns that were necessary for the garnering of his increasing wealth. O fool, fool,—for such the world will ever call thee,—thou art giving thyself trouble over a future which thou shalt never see! Thou art saying what thou wilt do, how thou wilt meet thy coming days when from the lips of Him in whose hands thy breath is, there has already gone

forth the word, "This night thy soul shall be required of thee."

I see those others also—a moving, flying picture of the same truth. As the train dashes onward, how many hearts within it are full of anxiety
for the morrow! "If my health should continue to
grow worse," says one within his heart, "I shall be
obliged to give up my business, and then what will
my poor family do?" Another is fearing and
troubled lest the sickness of his wife should prove
fatal and he be left with motherless children to care
for. Still another is in distress for fear the investment which is all his fortune shall prove unsound
and he be left in poverty and want.

So throughout the train—anxiety for the morrow fills human hearts, furrows human faces, when
suddenly a lurch, a plunge, a crash, a mass of
dying groans, and a score of these anxious human
souls are flying Godward, all thoughts of earth's
to-morrow forever out of their minds.

This also is true. The future may be much
brighter than the anxiety of human hearts depicts.
You who fear an early death may see your four-
score years. Health may be waiting for you who
fear a lifelong invalidism. The difficulties which
you think you see in your future pathway may be
only clumps of mist which will resolve themselves

and disappear as you draw closer. The lions may be chained. You may find that everything is for you instead of everything being against you. You may come upon joy when you expect sorrow; meet with success when you anticipate failure; come out upon a broad, smooth current where you have marked down the shooting rapids and the fearful falls. At least this much is true: your future is altogether unknown to you, and no anxiety on your part can prepare you for it.

So Jesus reasons when to-day He speaks unto you to say, " Be not anxious for the morrow." But He does not stop with this argument; He does not rest His case with your heart upon this showing. Beyond this He goes into that which He makes His great and characteristic argument with the anxious soul of man—viz., the measureless and unfailing love of the Father which is in heaven. Without this, poor and weak would have been His case. Our impotency, our ignorance would be a poor schoolmaster to bring us unto trust—poor comfort to wrap round our fearing hearts unless they also were themselves wrapped round about with the love which is quick to pity and able to save.

The fundamental, the all-conditioning fact of our world and of the universe is the existence of the

infinite God, and the fundamental truth concerning this infinite God is that He is a benignant
power. He is the Father of all the children of
earth and time; His highest, His all-inclusive
name is Love; and this love throned in the heavens is the great, the unanswerable argument against
the anxiety that furrows the face and consumes
the heart of His human child. If this love did
not exist, if it might fail, vain would it be to plead
the ignorance and the helplessness of the human
life—vain the attempt to mention any other or all
other reasons for the dismission of anxiety and
fear. If the completeness of infinite love flowed
not out unto our incompleteness, then we might
well worry and fear all our earthly days. If a
frown might gather upon that face which is the
light of the universe, then would every human
heart have good reason for the apprehension of
evil, for at any moment this frown might fall as
night upon the joy and the hope of man. If a
malignant thought might lift its dark form upward
in that heart whose pulsations feed all life and
being, then might every creature life reach out
with fear and trembling for the future, for that
wrathful thought might at any moment drive as
a thunderbolt through the home and the joy of
the soul.

But this we know from Jesus' lips can never be. Love it is that illumines the face that from the depths looks out upon man and the world, and love shall beautify its features forever. Love it is that fills the heart that feeds the stream of human hope, and this love in an endless current shall flow forth unto all creature need. This, then, is the great, the supreme argument against anxiety which Jesus makes with you to-day—viz.: Will you not trust your future in the hands of the infinite Love? Will you not, as a child, calmly commit yourself unto the care of the almighty and all-loving Father? Will you not, as you look forth upon the long, long path by which you go, let your heart have expression in this triumph of faith?

> " I know not what the future hath
>   Of marvel or surprise ;
>   Assured alone, that life and death
>   His mercy underlies."

That you may be able to fill your heart with a measure of this blessed confidence, Jesus asks you to look forth upon the broad fields whereon in illuminated characters is written the demonstration of an overruling power and a Divine care. Listen to His words and His argument: "Behold the fowls of the air: for they sow not, neither do they reap. . . Yet your heavenly Father feedeth them." Oh, ye anxious ones, can you not believe that you are much better than the fowls, much worthier of the Divine care, much surer of receiving it?

Look forth again, and, while you look, listen still to the Saviour's voice of interpretation. " Consider the lilies of the field, how they grow; they toil not, neither do they spin: And yet I say unto you, That even Solomon in all his glory was not arrayed like one of these." Oh! ye whose hearts are filled with anxiety for the morrow, can you not while you look and while you listen make your own this sweet inference which Jesus voices for you: " If, then, God so clothe the grass of the field, . . . shall He not much more clothe you, Oh! ye of little faith?"

Once more lift up your eyes upon the illuminated field, and may those eyes be opened that you may see.

Behold Calvary's stark and bitter cross flowing red with the blood of an infinite sacrifice! Draw closer to this Cross, that your eyes may be able to spell out these words that are written upon it: " If God spared not His own Son, but delivered Him up for us all, how shall He not with Him

also freely give us all things?" So we read
in letters each one of which is crimson with a
love that was unto death. So unto this glorious fullness rounds out the truth which the
Divine Teacher to-day gives unto you for the
rebuking and forbidding of your anxious heart.
Take it again, this divine argument, in all its completeness. The Feeder of the fowls, the Limner
of the lilies, the Giver of the Saviour—the future,
your future, is in the hands of this loving One, of
this great Care-taker, of this ungrudging and unceasing Giver, and you may safely trust Him
with it.

But all this, I know, may be truth only for the
head. What power shall give it unto the heart,
shall make it the inspiration, the strength and the
joy of earth's passing days? Many things seem
against us here, I know. Over the chamber door
of many of our hearts sits the raven form of in-
herited melancholy. The dregs of poisoned lives
run in our veins, and the specters of unbelief,
these also a birthmark, flit through our minds!
Then, besides, we live in a world full of anxiety
and fear, with care upon every side of us forevermore lifting up its horse-leech cry! Then, to
crown all, we have behind us, many of us, years
of living, so poor, so superficial, so false, so self-

6

seeking and self-trusting as almost to disable the power of beautiful faith. How can we, how can such as we, come unto peace? In such a world, and at the end of these selfish, restless, fearing, profitless days, how can we trust?

To all this I can reply only by saying that no unworthiness of the past shackles and imprisons our beautiful possibilities as children of the infinite Father. To all this I can reply only by saying there is a Divine Spirit whose office it is to take of the things of God and show them unto men, whose prerogative it is to shed abroad in human hearts the knowledge of the power of the Divine Love. To all this I can reply only by saying a man may be born when he is old, *so* old—born into the kingdom of God, born of the Spirit of God!

To this revealer of God and recreator of man, I pray you turn. Upon bended knees, beseech His inspiration, His interpretation of the Saviour's argument, His revelation of the Divine Love, His teaching of the lesson of the child's love and the child's trust.

My fellow-men, I come to you—unto you who believe in God as Father and Jesus Christ as Saviour—with this word of invitation: Trust God. Let the fowls of the air, always fed; let the grass of the field, always clothed; let the fall of the sparrow, always noted; let the cross of the Saviour, always luminous; let the sweet name of Father brought by Jesus from the skies, and now vocal in the air of earth, emphasize to you the invitation :—Trust God with your future! Oh, ye children of men whose flesh is often weak, whose hearts are often fearing, there is no one who loves you as God loves you, there is no one who yearns for your confidence as God yearns for it! Oh, ye whose hearts hold a bitterness with which a stranger may not intermeddle, and who along so many solitary paths are making your ways through life's darkness unto your little graves, there is One on high who is touched with the feeling of your infirmities, and to-day the minister plenipotentiary from this height of infinite love stands by your side and, pointing you down the long, long line of the morrows—the morrow of loss, the morrow of sorrow, the morrow of weakness, the morrow of pain, the morrow of death, the morrow of judgment, the morrow of immortality—speaks unto your heart to say: " Be not anxious, for, though you are weak, God is strong and good."

Be yours the answer of the helpless, loving, trusting child, the answer of trust which shall sing to sleep the doubts and the fears of your haunted

and restless hearts with the voice of this sweet
confidence. The future—my future—is in God's
hand, and love shall make the gift!

> And so beside the silent sea,
> I wait the muffled oar ;
> No harm from Him can come to me
> On ocean or on shore.
>
> I know not where His islands lift
> Their fronded palms in air ;
> I only know I cannot drift
> Beyond His love and care.

V

THE BIBLICAL SPECIES

V

THE BIBLICAL SPECIES

"The fool hath said in his heart, There is no God."—Ps. liii: 1.

THE Bible does not argue the existence of God. It takes this for granted, as it takes the being of man for granted, as it takes the existence of the material universe for granted. Its very first words are: "In the beginning God created the heaven and the earth."

Neither does the Bible ever stop to make explicit and positive assertion of the existence of God. This also it seems to regard as unnecessary, an affront to human reason, and a shame to the intuitions of the soul. But although it does not argue nor categorically assert the being of God, the Bible has now and then a word of irony and scorn for the atheism which is whispered in the heart or spoken by the life. The text is an example of the former; and I would have you at this time look into some very common and crystalline depths round about you, that so be, for the quickening of your faith, you may catch the glint of its bitter and beautiful scorn.

First of all, I ask you to gaze into the depths of the material universe.

This is unmeasured and immeasurable. It is unbounded; it is boundless. Take your stand upon the rounded surface of our globe and look into the celestial depths. You perceive no line of limitation; you can discover no outer edge; you can conceive even of no circumference. As far as the unassisted eye can reach, as far as the eagle eye of the telescope can penetrate; yea, as far as imagination can soar, it is the same un-changing vista—world upon world, sun upon sun, system upon system, in endless succession and with ever-increasing glory! Count the trees of the forest—there is a world for every one! Num-ber the flowers of the field—there is a sun for every one! Yea, count the millions of the human race, and then behold in the separating clusters of the Milky Way not only a sun, but a system for every individual life! Take the wings of the morning,—your chariot, the swift-winged light that girdles our globe eight times in a second,—and forty centuries shall have swept by you be-fore you reach yon shining point which is nightly telling to our earth the wondrous story of its birth. Make this jeweled stepping stone a new starting point; add four thousand years of more than lightning speed,—eight thousand years you have now traveled, new-darted with the light,—where is the circumference,—where the outer edge? Ah! if this is what you seek, you may as well turn backward in your flight, for immensity girts you in—that immensity of which every point is equally the center! Such is the material grandeur, the inconceivable vastness, the awful depths into which the man must look who says within his heart, "No God! No God!"

Take another point. All these worlds, all these suns, all these systems are swung in empty space, are hung upon nothing. Listen to the challenge as, breaking from the lips of an unseen speaker, it rings its bold sublimity in the ears of the patriarch of Uz: "Whereupon are the foundations of the earth fastened? Declare, if thou hast understanding!" Look about you! There is no unmoving point, no ponderous staple to which our earth is fastened. Momentarily transport yourself to the other hemisphere—there is no foundation upon which the world is builded! "Yea, He stretcheth the north over the empty place and hangeth the earth upon nothing."

Take another fact still. These worlds innumerable, these worlds hung all upon nothing, are all in motion, all sweeping forward with amazing velocity. Yet there is no collision, no jar, no sense of motion even! The whole universe, with not an atom of it at rest, and its motion music—upon this sublimely beautiful thought let your mind rest for a moment.

The moon revolves round our earth, the earth revolves upon its axis, while moon and earth sweep onward round the sun. The sun itself revolves, planet after planet wheel in well-appointed courses round him as their center, while at the same time earth, and heaven, and planets, and sun are sweeping forward, through unknown cycles, round a more sublime and imperious center still! Yet there is no collision, no jar, no uncertainty. We ourselves are the subjects of at least three well-defined and amazing motions, and yet there is no uncertainty in our steps, no ruffling of our garments, no disturbance of the most delicate machinery of our threefold being.

But I can dwell no longer upon this point. Upon this vast, immeasurable, baseless, whirring universe it is that the man must look who says within his heart, "No God! No God!" I appeal to you: Is not the Psalmist right when he lifts

his hand to brand the forehead of such an one
with the scorn of the text? Does not the deep,
clear voice of the human spirit—does not the
instinct of the human mind reach forth to under-
write the terrible verdict, and, with the living fire
of self-evident and necessary truth, to burn still
deeper the damnatory mark? This infinite expanse that encircles us, and which in immeasurable waves of insufferable splendor sweeps out
from us unto a circumference that is never
reached,—this mighty universe, in which our
earth is but an atom,—does it not take up the
declaration of the text and reëcho it throughout
all its upper and nether depths? This flying
immensity, whose flight is one unending song;
these august worlds and blazing suns, whose motion is a music that diadems the throne of law
with a corona of perpetual incense—do they not
catch up the reproach and, weaving it into their
never-ceasing watchword of glory to the Creator,
ring throughout all their infinite spaces the derisive words, "Thou worm! Thou fool!"

But let us continue our endeavor, not to demonstrate the existence of Deity, but to realize the
justification of the Psalmist's verdict, while we
turn to catch the glint of the scorn of the text in
and from Him who is earth's most prominent

object—at once its inhabitant, its possessor, and its Lord.

Here also I will name but three points—lift up before you but three capital truths.

First, man, " fearfully and wonderfully made."

Secondly, man, with a sense of dependence.

Thirdly, man, with a sense of accountability.

Enough there is in the first of these, even if I should omit the other two.

The human frame—its beauty, its unity, its complications; the mutual subserviency of all its members, their numberless adaptations and inter-dependencies; its system of electric nerves; its network of living channels; its bands of tendon and muscle; its manifold eye; its mysterious ear-gate; its organs of articulation, easily giving forth the sounds that call for half a thousand different adjustments with every passing moment; its instrument of all work, the thumb—Man, the up-right, walking, talking, rational, ruling form of earth's creation is enough to justify unto reason's ear forever the indignant scorn of the inspired writer.

But here we have only commenced. Think of the union of spirit and body; of mind and matter; of flesh and fire! Think of the immortal soul living, hiding within this tabernacle of flesh—

governing, guiding, inspiring this material frame; now sending its imperial mandate along the telegraphic nerve that a finger may be lifted; now ordering the contraction and now the expansion of a muscle; suffering through the body's hurts; joying through the body's health; disposing of all the physical forces as a general does of his troops, and sometimes, as if turned traitor, infuriating the hand which clutches the dagger which turns its frail companion to dust by the act of a suicide.

Centuries ago, a man whose eyes were opened looked upon all this and gave out his conclusion in these words: " I will praise Thee; for I am fearfully and wonderfully made." And while he was so wondering and praising, he heard by his side a human heart whispering into his ear the words, " No God! No God!" Was it strange that in such a case the impressed and reverent spirit should intermit its praises long enough to turn and exclaim: " No God, and yet so fearfully and wonderfully made—why, thou fool!"

But let us go farther.

There is a sense of dependence hidden within the depths of man's being. Listen to it as it breaks forth in the hour of sudden peril! Hear it as it mingles itself in sorrow's wail! Catch its accents, as in minor tones it pours itself through all languages and through all literatures! It is not peculiar to those who have received a religious education, but belongs to man as man. With all men, in all ranks, in all nationalities, in all ages it is found. The prayers of all the generations breathe it. The hymns of all the generations sing it. Thus its universality proves that this sense of consciousness is no artificial quality that has been bred into human nature, but an original endowment, a primal and necessary factor of human nature.

Now, if there is no Infinite One upon whom we may depend, what have we? Not a false and vicious habit bred into man, but a mocking delusion as one of the original elements of his being, a hideous lie woven into the very texture of the human soul. We have the flower turning its pale face as if sunward, and only a cold, blank nothingness to answer its sweet voice of worship and of trust. The tides lift up their mighty masses, as if in the enthusiasm of their loyalty they would pour out their very being upon a mighty orb, and as their answer hear only a thin and hollow voice calling out, "What do ye— there is nothing here?" We have the homing instinct of the bird, and no home!—the faith of the child, and no father!—the unescapable idea of God, and no God! Surely, if not worthy of a harder name, he is a fool who thus deals with the ineradicable consciousness of the human soul, and stamps our moral constitution a contradiction and a lie.

But further consider. All men have the idea of moral quality. They distinguish between the right and the wrong, and are compelled so to distinguish. I say not that the standard of right is uniform. It is not. What is right to one man or a nation is not always so to another individual or to a different race. But the sense of moral quality is universal. All classes, all individuals have their right and their wrong—divide human conduct into two categories, that which ought, and that which ought not to be done. And this is all that is asked for here—this universal and necessary idea of rightness, of obligation, of judgment condemnatory or approving, upon the acts that men perform. Consider, first, that this is universal. Consider, secondly, that being something which has not been bred into human nature, it is also something which cannot be bred out of human nature. A false education, the power of a bad life, the influence of a vicious environment, are able to oppose, to weaken. to silence this moral sense, but not to destroy it. Within the soul, enfeebled and silent though it be, it continues its existence, and in many ways gives evidence of its readiness at any future moment to reassert itself.

This moral sense—natural, universal, apparently deathless—what can it be but the impress of the infinite upon the finite; the echo of a divine voice within the human soul; the sentence of a great and final judge in ceaseless articulation? It is nonsense to cry out "superstition." As well shout "parallelogram!" There is no explanation in this word superstition. The question remains, How does it happen that human nature always takes on this particular form of delusion? Neither is it anything more than pompous verbosity to call this moral sense an eddy of the great stream of tendency, or the correlate of law. Law without a lawgiver is a misnomer and nonsense. There never was and there never can be such a law. Law is not force, but only a method of force, having power neither to originate nor to execute itself.

Look now at the matter as it stands. A sense within man says, there is such a thing as right and there is such a thing as wrong: the right ought to be done, and the wrong ought not to be done; do the right and it shall be well with you;

do the wrong and you shall suffer. These voices are coeval with the race of man, are unceasing, undying within the individual soul. What then is the necessary conclusion? What can it be but this? Man is under law, and this means man responsible to a lawgiver; and this again means, man accountable unto God. Yet within the heart, in which echo these deathless voices, there has been heard the whisper, "No God, No God!" Why this, surely, is man turning upon himself! This is the free agent saying with his own being—"Thou lie!" This is a manufactured whisper, lifted up against the involuntary and continuous testimony of all the moral powers, and surely he must be a fool who, by an effort of the will, gives birth and continuance and respect unto such an unnatural, interjected, and evermore reputed falsehood.

But again, you may catch the reflection of the scorn of the text from the surface and from out the depths of human history. Here also the necessity of the sermon compels brevity. I mention, first of all, the general progress of the realization of righteousness—a state of rightness—for earth and man. Surely this gleams from the bosom of the centuries. The march of what we know as the forces of civilization has been an onward march. See this in the growth and spread of civil and religious liberty; in the emancipation of woman; in the uplifting of the poor; in the enlargement of the common man; in the countless forms of charity, which, crystallizing in most beautiful shapes, fairly bestud the crown of earth, as stars the crown of night; in the ten thousand forms of merciful alleviation, which with ever-increasing number and efficiency are working for the amelioration of human suffering, and for the righting of human wrong.

Slow, do you say? I care not to argue over this word " slow." We are but creatures of a day —yesterday in our cradle and to-morrow in our grave—and are not, perhaps, good judges of what is slow and what is rapid, in the progress of the forces of an infinite realm, and an eternal kingdom. All that I desire that you should recognize and admit here, is the power which is working for righteousness in this world—the tidal force which is pushing the waters of a regenerating influence farther and still farther into the continent of human sorrow and of human sin. " Man "—do you cry out? Human agency, all this? Why it originated in a world that needed it, but which on account of this need could not and did not desire it. It has been carried forward in days and through centuries where no love of it, and no purposeful coöperation with it, was to be found in heart of man or power of earth.

I mention, secondly, remarkable interpositions in human history—patent *ab-extra* and dominating influences.

"To the Nile, with your fore-doomed child," spoke the voice of earth's mightiest Power to a poor Hebrew mother, centuries ago. The slave-mother obeyed, and in obeying placed her child in the arms of Pharaoh's daughter, to be nourished as Israel's deliverer. And this is but a typical case. Frequently in the history of the world have human wisdom and human power wrought out the confusion and overthrow of their most dearly cherished plans. Babels have been resolved upon and never builded; persecutors have scattered the seeds of the life that was to be stamped out; human slavery has been extinguished by means resolved upon by the most astute political wisdom for its extension and defense; the wrath of man has praised, not himself, but an unseen power which stood in his pathway with a flaming sword.

Besides the general progress of the world, and this supernaturally adroit interposition into human history, I mention one conspicuous, salient fact, viz., the Christian Church. This was founded by one Jesus of Nazareth, a carpenter's son, born in a stable in Bethlehem of Judæa, poor, despised, absolutely destitute of every species of human influence, and whose life was, at the last, swept from the earth's surface by an ignominious death. This religion was promulgated by a band of twelve disciples, all but one of whom were illiterate men. It has nothing in it, either in the duties that it enjoins, or in the rewards that it promises, to allure the ambition or to gratify the passions of man.

Yet it has lived, yet it has grown, shaping civilizations, building nations, marshaling the mightiest forces of time. Mohammedanism, that flashed upon the world with the light of its drawn sword, now grows paler and paler with the increasing dimness of this sword, and even with the hope of its sensual paradise is now able to kindle but a feeble fire of loyalty within the earth. But nineteen hundred years have passed, and now no longer oriental, but occidental as well, the Christian Church marches in the van of the world's progress, and is incontestably the most vital, the most extended, the most modern, the most powerful of all the forces that to-day are shaping the history of our globe.

But here again I pause. What shall we say? That the past centuries cry aloud there is a God? Yes, surely this. But this is a weak translation of their testimony. Let us give the witness nobler, worthier voice. As its gulf stream of progress, distinctly visible through all the currents and counter-currents of the past, cuts its way onward with a force which no human power may stay or divert; as its ten thousand marvelous conjunctions and issues which no human intelligence conceived and no human power wrought out, lift themselves up in luminous array, history, scorning to be set forth as the proof of a necessary and self-evident truth, fairly thunders forth this voice : "The man who, even in his heart, dares to say, no God! no God!—let him be called a fool and all the centuries shall cry, Amen."

But once more.

Let us justify unto ourselves the bold language of the text by a glance unto Him who is the central figure among all time's millions, the personality round whom all time's centuries revolve— Jesus of Nazareth.

Take the Sermon on the Mount. Was such teaching current, was it possible, in the day and nation in which Jesus lived? The answer cannot be kept back or changed: "Never man spake like this man." In method—its calm, undoubting, yet gentlest dogmatism; in the elevation of its tone—its moral sublimity; in its majestic breadth—its application to all days and to all men —it was supernatural, something that was not born of that age, but which descended upon it, was let down into it.

Then look unto and mark the breadth of Jesus' character and sympathies.

Remember that He belonged to the narrowest, the most exclusive people on the face of the earth; yet in His sympathies and hopes He embraced the world, and all His words and doctrines are current coin in the twentieth century and in the land of the setting sun. Jesus still leads in the world's progress. The carpenter's Son is, unto this day, *facile princeps* among the world's great reformers. Can any thoughtful mind receive this, and then say, "Man is at the head—there is nothing above man"?

Consider further the surpernatural beauty of His character. In that far-off, narrow, bigoted, selfish, cruel day, behold Him walking unspotted, stainless, loving—the Man of the seamless robe, set not only above that day, but above all earth's days and men. That light, that radiance, that unmatched beauty, that corona of unapproached goodness, was it merely, only human? As well affirm that the unsufferable splendor of yonder sun is but our earth's reflected light. Oh, no! The eyes that look upon the Man of Palestine behold a brightness more than human, look upon a light that has never gilded land or sea in all the centuries of human evolution. He is the manifestation of an unseen glory; the outraying of an infinite excellence, which would thus become the light of the world, the light and the life of men.

The glance within, the glance without, meet the glint of the text. The Psalmist was none too bold, his scorn none too incisive. He but spoke the plain and solemn truth when he said he is a fool who says within his heart, No God, no God. Here let me affirm, that the day for calling things by their right names shall not always be postponed. "This thing was not done in a corner." A day of light has dawned upon our world and human lives are passing forward into it. Now is the judgment of this world, and human lives are haled unto this judgment. It is a day of God in which we live, and human souls must meet Him in it. There is no escape from this issue and from this demonstration. No hu-

man mind may ignore or belittle the primal fact
and basal truth of the universe, and for long
pass as a profound thinker. The agnosticism
which is virtual atheism shall not always be regarded as proof presumptive of mental breadth
and power. The living soul of the universe shall
break forth upon the human spirit. "A God!"
the heavens shall cry. "A God!" the earth reply.
In this bursting light in the apocalypse of the one
all-inclusive Reality, in this blazing forth of the
Infinite, whither shall run or in what dark corner hide, the puny, presuming creature-life, which
dared to wear as its crown that know-nothingism
which is the scorn of the mind's highest reach,
and the contempt of the soul's sweetest inspiration? Wherever he may flee or wherever hide,
truth's living light shall dart after him to burn
deep, and still deeper into his forehead the words
of this merciless condemnation: "Professing himself to be wise, this man became a fool."

Only one word more. If the scorn of the text
justly lies against the one who says in his heart,
"No God," must it not also apply and with cumu-
lative force to the man who in and by his life says
"There is no God"? This is a form of the athe-
istic lie which is upon every side of us. Different
classes of human lives are continually crying it

into our ears. Let me mention some of these classes.

First, the sensual type—the intemperate, the licentious. If there is a God, He must abhor this human filth. Therefore, this class, the impure, the dissolute, by their lives are shouting out the words, " No God, no God."

Secondly, the irreverent type. Human lives for twenty, forty, four score years walk the wondrous earth-path that takes its way over the rounded surface of a flying world beneath the mighty arch of the skies ; live all these years girt in with inconceivable wonder on every hand ; fairly deluged with evidences of supernal power and immeasurable wisdom, and drop at length into the darkness of the grave, non-worshipers, without once having bowed their souls before the infinities of wisdom and power that were blazoned forth before their eyes. Surely this is living as if there was no God.

Thirdly, the self-centered, the utterly selfish type. Men and women there are in every city, by the score, to whom money has come by inheritance, or through the talents bestowed upon them, or the opportunities offered to them, who are spending this money, and all this money, upon themselves, and only upon themselves.

They build the new and spacious mansion; they clothe themselves in gorgeous apparel; they take the summer voyage and the winter excursion, and this year after year, just as if there was no want or suffering within the world—just as if they did not belong to a brotherhood many of whose members are ignorant and poor and cold and hungry. Surely again, if infinite Love delights in the service of her needy children, this is living as if there was no God. Surely again, life here is one bold, shameless word, thrust into the ears of men, and into the face of heaven—this one, bold, shameless word, " No God! no God!"

So by actions, that speak louder than words, are human lives shouting upon every side of us the affirmation of the heart against which the text directs its scorn. Men ignore duty. When the call is unto worship, they do not bow. When the command is for obedience, they lift up self-will as their highest law. So are men everywhere, in the light of this twentieth century of Christ, saying, not in heart-whispers, but in the outspoken voice of conduct, " No God—no God."

Here, by the deep, full heavens into which men look; by the sense of dependence and accountability that stirs within the human heart; by the luminous path of human progress that reaches through the centuries unto the present day; and by the beautiful Christ who evermore is lifted up before human eyes, I protest against this atheism of the life, and prophesy the breaking of a day, which shall turn the blush of shame into its cheek, and in the light of a demonstration which shall justify the coronation, shall place upon its head a blacker crown than that which, centuries ago, was fashioned for the atheism of the heart.

V I

SPIRITUAL NOVELTIES

VI

SPIRITUAL NOVELTIES

" But the word of the Lord endureth for ever. And this is the word which by the gospel is preached unto you."—1 Peter 1 : 25.

BOTH those who applaud and those who deplore it, will do well to remember that the mental restlessness of the present day is no new thing under the sun. If you will turn back nineteen hundred years, you will hear the apostle Paul exhorting his spiritual son in these words : " Avoid oppositions of science, falsely so-called, which some professing have erred from the faith." Is not this a very good photograph of many a twentieth-century man, who in gaining a little science has lost all his religion ? Behold also the same fact illustrated in one of the freshest crazes of our day. This cult, which announces itself as the incorporated unity of science and religion, is shown to be very near of kin to a strange first-century species, for we hear the same great apostle warning against a certain class of leaders and teachers in these words : " For of this sort are they which creep into houses, and lead captive silly women." Surely the adjec-

tive here is **not** an inapt description of those in
our day who accept as Christian Science a jumble
that ignores the imperatives of both the great realms
whose names are invoked. I may add par-
enthetically in passing, that the only reason,
doubtless, why the apostle made this character-
ization of one sex only, was because the leisure
class was nonexistent among those to whom he
wrote, and that the men of that day avoided the
fate of some of their twentieth-century brothers
by being out at their daily tasks, saved, as so
many have been since that far-away time, by the
blessed necessity of work.

Then, if you look back into history as far as
unto Athen's pride and Athen's glory, you will
discover a large class who "spend their time in
nothing else, but either to tell or to hear some
new thing." Now beyond question this is an ac-
curate description of a certain type of intellectual
life which in our day both delights and distresses
the souls of the children of men. If, therefore, the
passion or itching for novelty is a proof of intel-
lectuality, then the first century was intellectual as
truly as the twentieth, and if this craze is the condition and the sign of progress, then those who lived
in Paul's day share with us the glory of furnishing
this condition and of lifting up this sign. So I say

unto you who are holding on to faith with a sad and almost despairing courage, because of the mental restlessness round about you, that this is no new thing upon which you look; no new power of temptation that you feel; neither does it betoken a spiritual cataclysm or the end of faith in the earth. I also say unto you who are congratulating yourselves upon your participation in the present skepticism, as if it were the crown of earth's last and opening century, that the soil of every generation beneath your feet is full of the dust of those who, while in human form, were " ever learning, and never able to come to the knowledge of the truth." There has not been in the past centuries such a wonderful unlikeness between the spirit of earth's different days, the spirit that has breathed upon human hearts and seduced human lives. There are more minds of the skeptical type than ever before, but this is only because there are more people in the world. The proportion of restless minds and unbelieving souls, I apprehend, has not greatly changed.

But whatever the spirit of the day, the responsibility of the individual remains, for it is the spirit of a man, and not of a day, that passes forward unto judgment. If this man gulps down whatever is offered him, he may swallow poison whether in

8

the first or twentieth century. If he dances to whatever tune is played, he may dance into hell from the floor of any century or of any day.

I ask your attention to some of the false assumptions bound up within the craze for novelty in the spiritual realm—a craze, let me add, as old as Athens and as young as Buffalo.

I. The first of these assumptions is this : Modern progress has discredited the old things of Christian faith.

The progress of our world within the last fifty years is unspeakably marvelous. No human tongue can overspeak or overpraise it. If only we are careful to note the field in which it has brought forth its wonders, we shall all do well to join most enthusiastically with those who magnify and glorify the present day. But this careful marking of the field of modern-day wonders has not always been done. From progress in one or many directions, by a *non sequitur* progress in every direction has been inferred. So it has happened that even in the spiritual realm, the cry of progress has been taken up and reëchoed until many have actually come to believe that this progress has sounded the death knell of all the old things of Christian faith. But indeed nothing is plainer than that this marvelous and worthily vaunted progress has not touched one of these things.

Let me prove this to you by a very simple illustration. Suppose that to-day you should be called to the bedside of a dying man. Let churches and creeds and all formal religion now drop out of sight. Let the case be simply this. The dying man is a friend of yours, whom you would kindly and faithfully serve. Now as you stand in the shadows of the solemn hour, with his hungry, appealing eyes upon you, what new word of twentieth-century truth, what new watchword of twentieth-century origin, have you for your passing friend? Will you tell him that he is but meeting the inevitable? Ah! he knows this without your saying it, and besides, any heathen philosopher, thousands of years ago, could have told him this much. Will you go further and tell him that the power in whose hands he lies is a power of love? Is this all you have for your friend? Why, a John and a Paul centuries ago were able to say this much and often did say it. Will you go still further and say unto your friend, "There is a divine Saviour who will walk with you through the dark valley"? Why, David, centuries before the Christ, could and did say as much as that. Where then is the proof of progress in the spiritual realm, if it has nothing new to offer, if it is silent in the hour when human love would fain serve human extremity?

Or let the form of the illustration be a little changed. Suppose that with the deepening shadows of this holy day the angel of death should suddenly appear beckoning to *you*. I will make the most favorable supposition of your case. You have, say, lived in a circle of the world's most advanced thought. You have heard and read much learnedly critical of the old faith, and eloquently extolling the new and broader day unto which humanity has come. As you have listened to their words of glorification and repudiation, you have often said within your heart—sometimes with your lips—" Yes, it is a new and wonderful day! The old things of Christian faith have fled away before the rising and spreading light!"

So you have lived and imagined and spoken. Now, you and this much glorified day of progress meet in what is to you an hour of sorest need, when you feel the damp dews gathering on your brow, and the human heart fainting within your breast. Turn now to your new and broad day of light to receive from its hand its especial gift unto your necessity!

What is this gift? A new God? No. A new map of the death-valley? No. A new vision of the land immortal? No. A new watchword to ring out cheer and courage in the black darkness that is falling upon you? No. What is then the gift of the much glorified progress unto you who have so often spoken its praises? An interrogation point—illuminated it may be by the hand of culture—but still only an interrogation point. This is the gift of modern progress unto your sore need, this is the unction with which she runs unto you—a dying man. If you were called upon to die to-day, you would have to die as the brute, without faith and without thought, or you would be obliged to pillow your fainting spirit upon the old truths of the old Bible—upon the Father whom Jesus taught in the first century, upon the grace of that Saviour whose cross is nineteen hundred years old.

Where then is the glory or the fact of modern progress in the spiritual realm, if it has nothing new in the way of knowledge, or comfort, or courage, or cheer for a man in the hour of his supremest need?

Yet human voices all about us go on shouting progress, as if all the old things of religion had been discredited and abolished. I pray you in this hour put your fingers in your ears, shut out the noisy and popular shouts of humanity's progress long enough to read and to learn the exact truth of the case. There has been no progress in the spiritual realm, save that of word-emphasis. Not a light of all the thousands that sparkled in the great Columbian Exposition threw down a single new ray upon the path by which a man goes out of this world. There was not in all that forest of inventions a single one to explain life, to set forth God, to make soft the bed of death. Among all the exhibits by which the French Capital celebrated the incoming of the twentieth century, there was not one from that world into which human lives are pouring at the rate of one hundred thousand with every passing day. In the third great Exposition, the rainbow city—fair as the new Jerusalem descending out of heaven, which, as if at the wand of some supernal power, sprang into illumined and inimitable beauty upon the shores of Lake Erie—the record was the same. Upon life, spirit, God, the world to come, nothing new—no new exhibit. The secret and the spirit of Niagara blossomed into ten thousand times ten thousand lights, but the spirit and the secret of that world unto which sweep the millions of earth made no new showing of themselves.

The old things of religion, discredited, superseded, abolished! Why, not one of them has been touched! About God and soul-life, about the first great cause and the end which waits; about evil, its entrance into the world and its future history; concerning Jesus Christ and His proffered aid to man; concerning the future life and the condition of human immortality—about all these things we know no more than did the disciples of Paul nineteen hundred years ago. What Macaulay wrote years ago still remains true—a first-century man with a Bible in his hand is the equal of the nineteenth-century man, so far as spiritual knowledge is concerned. All the logomachies that have raged round religion's great verities have left them just where they were on the day that the Isle of Patmos saw the venerable seer affix the memorable seal. There have been speculations numberless, but no new discoveries; an endless succession of discussion but no new knowledge. The intuition of God, the origin and destiny of man, the vision of the Christ, the consciousness of sin, the intimation of immortality—these fundamentals remain as they were in the days of Paul, and the assumption that modern progress has invalidated them, or brought in any substitute for them, is a great delusion wrought into the pride and folly of the Athenian mind.

II. A second false assumption wrought into the craze for spiritual novelty is this: Mental restlessness is in itself so much progress.

There are many who seem to think that just because they have cut loose from the old anchorage of faith, therefore they have been thinking, and thinking to a purpose. But is this true? Is motion necessarily progress? Is activity necessarily profitable activity? Is drifting the same as making a voyage? Haul up the anchor, cut the hawser, and the vessel will begin to move, it is true. But what of this? Such a vessel, as likely as not, will whirl round and round in an eddy of wave and foam; she will float out with the tide or in with the tide; but in either case there is no progress, nothing but an idle swash and profitless churning of the waters.

And the moral world holds many such crafts within it. Derelicts they are, going nowhere themselves and only endangering the progress of the soul that is seeking some desired haven. Lift a wagon wheel from the ground and you may spin it round and round, but it will go no whither. It may revolve with great demonstration, and startle the onlookers with the smoke of its heated axle, but all this means only so much useless wear and tear. There is in it all neither profit nor promise. So in the spiritual world, when human minds are lifted up from the solid ground of revealed truth. They may make a great whirring with their " Lo ! here, lo ! there !" but all the same they will make no progress. Air plants they are, the victims of self-levitation, feeding upon the thin nutriment of their own guesses; windmills beating the air exhaled from their own lungs; and their record in our day and in all days makes it very clear that mental activity is not necessarily profitable activity, that mental drifting is not one and the same thing with spiritual progress.

Suppose a man has closed or thrown away the Bible, or that under the influence of modern criticism has taken it down from its high and solitary preëminence. But the Bible did not invent sin, or sorrow, or suffering, or death, and after it has been discarded these things will remain, and the soul of man will still need some authoritative voice upon them. Say that a human hand has put away the Christ; but still the human life remains consciously weak, with darkness all around it and greater darkness before it. Will not this life need some hope, some helper to take the place of the rejected Saviour?

No, no! Mental restlessness, spiritual drifting,— these are not necessarily so much progress. Because the old has been cast away, this does not mean that something better has been found to take its place, and the assumption that it does is a baleful error hiding within the glorified inertia of the Athenian mind.

III. A third false assumption bound up in the passion for spiritual novelty is this: Skepticism is the highest form of intellectual life. The word culture—spelled with a big C—has proved itself in our day and in all days a veritable Moloch unto which many poor souls have passed both the intuitions of their spirits and the precious word of God which was within their hands. I cannot think that I overstate the truth when I add, that the sensational demonstration that attends upon skepticism has had something to do in bringing about this strange and sad state of things. We live, you know, in a newspaper day. The world has had its age of stone, and of brass, and now it has its newspaper day—also one of brass. You well know what prominence this species of world activity gives to the unusual, the abnormal. One mad dog running down the street, snapping at everything in its way, is worth more to a newspaper than a hundred beautiful and noble specimens of the same species that are not rabid. One runaway horse, smashing things as he goes, is preferred above the thousands of the gentle type, which in the beauty and quietness of useful service do the work of the whole city. So one professor, kicking over the traces and threatening the safety of the whole theological establishment, is given larger place in the daily press than all the remaining members of the Faculty.

This sure expectation of fame, it cannot well be doubted, has seduced a few at the front, and these have drawn after them a large crowd of the uneducated, the unstable, and the irreverent, who cease not to split their throats with the cry, "Bravo! bravo! great is he that cometh in the name of the critic. What a scholar is this who is not afraid to lay his hands upon that which all the Christian centuries have regarded as sacred! No back number this one, but an up-to-date man."

So the professor's egoism is gratified, and so there flock to hear the preacher those who would not go near him were he emphasizing instead of criticizing the Bible. So it has come to pass that you cannot throw a stone to-day without

hitting some one, now an editor, now a professor, and now a preacher, whom the crowd of
the Adullamites have canonized for his free and
irreverent handling of the old things of faith and
hope.

But criticism is always easy. Destruction is a
much simpler matter than construction. It took
a genius to rear the Ephesian dome, but any
fool could apply the torch to it. Rejection, too,
is not necessarily the sign of strength. When
the stomach throws up its food, this is not always because it is strong, but as often because
it is weak. Neither is rejection always the sign
of benevolence. A soured, or envious, or cynical
soul, under the guise of liberality and public service, may do the throwing out here. Only a few
great souls—you can count them on your fingers
—have ever constructed any faith for mankind,
but the woods and the plains are full of com-
moners, who have snapped at, and carped at, and
spit upon the priceless treasures of the soul's inspiration and the soul's hope. Only a small minority
of the world's millions have endured as seeing Him
who is invisible, but the crust of the earth is
thick with the ashes, and the surface of the earth is
black with the shadows, of those who have smirked
and grinned in the face of supernal reality, who, as

the browsing ox upon the glories of the sunset sky, have turned their supercilious gaze upon the immensities and the eternities, only to say, "I see nothing there—there is nothing there." Believe me, my fellow-men, it is the easiest thing in the world to let go of supersensual realities. The world laughs at the mental grasp here—sin benumbs the fingers and the devil unclasps them. There are few of the modern world's millionaires who remain humble and spiritual; there is not a large proportion of politicians who see in the Ten Commandments anything more than an iridescent dream: there is not a surprisingly large number of the children of leisure, of fashion, and of wealth who walk before God in truth and purity and simplicity. No! such faith calls for ceaseless vigilance: for a strenuous denial of the lower forms of appetite and self-will, for unfailing spiritual aspiration, and the assumption that the inertia of the human mind that spends all its time in hearing or in telling some new thing is a sure sign of mental strength and high culture is one of the silliest delusions that the father of lies has ever palmed off upon a human soul, or with which he has ever befogged an earth-born day.

IV. But there is a fourth false assumption that

hides within the craze for novelty in the spiritual realm, to which, in closing, I must briefly advert. It is this: Man has so changed, the world has so changed as to render the word of the old gospel insufficient, inapplicable, and obsolete.

The constituent thought here is, that Jesus did not anticipate the character and extent of modern progress. When He spoke to the world He did not anticipate the scientific development that was to come: did not foresee the day when men would wing their words and propel their bodies with the lightning of heaven: had no vision of the coming man who was to be the possessor of two hundred millions of dollars: had no prevision of the day of universal education, of the multiform discoveries and the new knowledge which were to crown in glory the twentieth century. He spoke a word true enough and good enough for the then little world of man—but for the new and broader day unto which humanity has come, there must be a new and a broader gospel.

This, you will note, is a very bold assumption. It is nothing less than to charge Jesus the Christ with provincialism; to affirm that He was the creature of the day in which He lived, not broader than this day, not seeing beyond it.

But bold as the insinuation is, it is as fallacious as it is bold.

Man has not so greatly changed since the day of Jesus and of Paul. Even his body has not come unto any novelty of life-function. The circulation of the blood, the process of digestion, the action of the nervous system, these are exactly what they were nineteen centuries ago. The human body now takes its food from a table very unlike that which was spread in the first century, but its nourishment and growth are by the same laws, maturity comes in the same manner, and death follows in the same old way. In the spiritual man also there has been no deep or radical change.

Take the last and most characteristic product here—the man of the twentieth century. A thorough-going man of the world let him be, a multimillionaire, if you please, member of a dozen clubs and of a hundred corporations, owner of a railroad that spans a continent and of a steamship line that bridges the great ocean, with material relations and civic responsibilities and communal functions of which the first century never dreamed! As you look upon this wonderful product of to-day, maybe you are ready to exclaim: " What a different being from the simple fisherman, from the rude shepherd to whom Jesus spoke and with whom Jesus consorted! The old gospel will not do for this new man."

But in reality the difference that amazes you here is only in accidentals, only in evanescent externals, only in the man's clothes, whether these clothes be the garments that cover his body, or the palace in which he lives, or the multitudinous trappings of sense that jingle along his earthly pathway. In a single hour all these distinguishing accidents shall drop from the twentieth-century life, and it will show itself unto the world and unto the universe as a weak, suffering, dying man! Only this and nothing more. Only this, and in this ultimate reduction and final analysis, the wonderful product of earth's last day will reproduce without the change of a single feature the man of the first century. He will draw out of a room of greater money value than a whole province of Palestine in Jesus' day, but he will draw out of this palatial environment in as simple a form, as empty-handed, as naked, as helpless as twenty centuries ago the human life drew out of the shepherd's tent or the fisherman's hut. How superficial, how foolish then the assumption that this modern twentieth-century conglomerate, in the center of which is the unchanged human spirit, needs any new word, any new gospel from the unchanging God! As if there must be a new evangel for the larger pile of goods; for the longer bank account; for the railway; for the steamship line! As if these things were a part of the man!

Receive in conclusion, I pray you, these two inferential and applicatory thoughts.

First, the pitiableness of the hysteric craze for spiritual novelty. Pitiable for two reasons. First, because it is the attempt of the human intellect, usurping the prerogatives of intuition and of revelation, to make discovery in a realm which is hopelessly beyond its reach. The man might as well say, "I am looking into the fauna and flora of Neptune," as to say "I am investigating the problems of evil, of spirit, of God, of immortality." Here also professing himself to be wise, the man quickly becomes, and most sadly, a fool.

Pitiable also is this craze, for it is the denial to the poor human heart amid the contradictions, and troubles, and sorrows of the present life, of the comfort and inspiration of accepted and unchanging truth.

The second application of this whole subject is this: Reason's high obligation and faith's fine opportunity.

Our day confuses man's temporal functions

with his immortal life. It is as if into the presence of the sick man there should gather a company of his friends to discuss what uniform he
shall wear, what business he shall take up, what
social or civic responsibilities he shall assume—
and in the meantime the man is dying! So those
who are wise above that which is written, "the
foolish prophets, that follow their own spirit, and
have seen nothing," gather themselves into the
spiritual sanctuary to discuss social economics;
to formulate theories concerning spiritual myster-
ies; to guess at what the world's crowd shall be
and do! And this while the human life through
sorrow, through suffering, and through death is
moving forward unto judgment!

There is but one great question that spiritual
truth needs to answer in time's day, and this is
the redemption, the safety of time's one great
entity—the individual man. This secured, earth
will be cared for, and heaven will not lose its own.
The truth which conditions this great issue has
been given unto the world, and is as unchanging
as the immutable God or His eternal throne:
"This is life eternal, to know Thee, the only
true God, and Jesus Christ, whom Thou hast
sent."

"The word of the Lord endureth forever. And

this is the word which by the gospel is preached unto you."

My fellow-men, you who are immortal citizens of the kingdom of God, if you have any respect for yourselves, for your worthiness and your dignity; if you have any reverence for the beauty and majesty and glory of the infinite realm, I beseech you, that with a beautiful contempt you spurn from you the foolish and ephemeral spiritual novelties of the Athenian or the Yankee mind, and bow with all reverence in the presence of the unchanging word that conditions the redemption of man and the regeneration of the world. So preserving both self-respect and faith in Him who is the God of things as they are, through Him who is time's apocalypse of this reality, you shall have cause to render thankful praises while thought or being lasts or immortality endures.

VII

THE SIFTING OF THE SENSUOUS LIFE

VII

THE SIFTING OF THE SENSUOUS LIFE

"And Jacob was left alone; and there wrestled a man with him until the breaking of the day."—Gen. xxxii : 24.

JACOB was a smart, shrewd, successful man. If there had been newspapers in that far-off day, he would have been referred to as our rising young townsman, our eminent citizen. He was smart enough, with the aid of his wily mother, to entrap and to rob his brother Esau, and when driven from home by this sharp practice he was shrewd enough to so manage things as to increase his own holdings at the expense of his trusting and generous uncle. And now with all the property that he had accumulated while in residence with this uncle—with all his oxen and asses and flocks, with his men-servants and women-servants—he turns his face toward his old home, turns from the scenes of his business success and fortune-getting, to run into the hour which should thoroughly sift his inward life, which should make him afraid and ashamed of that which he had come to regard as his success, his fortune, and his glory.

Let us note how this crucial hour breaks upon the head of such a life : First of all, in the revelation of the reality, the nearness, the overwhelming importance of an unseen world to which the human life most truly and everlastingly belongs. We live upon the rounded surface of a flying ball, out from which in any direction space sweeps away in distances unmeasured and unmeasurable. In a vast universe, to which even imagination can set no bounds, is plunged and wheels forward the world upon which we have our home and all that we call ours. This rimless reservoir, these depths, these heights, these stretches of space are but as vacancy to many of the hours of the human life. Men see nothing in them; they feel nothing from them. The channels of the senses flood the mind and fill the heart, and outside of the territory which these drain the human life penetrates not at all.

The sensuous spirit, the fleshly life, walks in the presence of the vast infinite, and knows no connection with it. Its world, its universe, is the office, the shop, the home. The pleasure which allures, the gain which is sought, the ambition which dominates—the human lives that pass and repass, that laugh and cry, that suffer and die— this is reality, this is the all to many an hour of

the human life. Ask the man in such an hour
what he sees in yonder depths, and your answer
shall be a stare, or a sneer, or a pitying smile.
Yes! but over the head of this sensuous life may
at any time break an hour which shall bring the
sentient, thrilling spirit into vital connection with
that which now seems emptiness and void. A few
hours ago his family, his servants, his cattle seemed
to Jacob to fill the spaces by Jabbok's ford. Now
these all are gone, and yet they leave not emptiness
behind them. There is that remaining with which
Jacob may have communion—with which he may,
must, wrestle. Jabbok's ford is still tenanted. So
sweep away from the world-absorbed soul its
environment of the material, so isolate the sensuous spirit, and out of the desert of sense so created
reality shall speak unto the human life, and unseen
Being hold mysterious communion with the solitary human spirit.

The hour of danger even more surely and
more vividly than the hour of loneliness makes
the same revelation. Behold the supplanter by
Jabbok's ford! It is an hour in which everything
that he holds dear—the safety of his family, the
lives of his dependents, the fruit of twenty years
of toil—all are at stake. Suddenly, as the sand-
cloud of the desert rises up in the path of the

caravan, there is lifted up before Jacob the wrathful cloud of four hundred armed men, and in the
midst of this cloud, and glaring out upon him from
its blackness, the face of his wronged brother
Esau. What shall be the result? Shall the angry
cloud tear a path of ruin through his possessions?
Shall a cruel death sweep from before his very
eyes the forms of his loved ones? The hour is
critical and the smart and successful man trembles
before it. No sooner is he alone in the presence
of his danger than the void about him grows
tremulous, palpitating with life, and he himself is
wrestling with that which to a lighter hour had
been vacancy and nothingness. So ever does the
hour of sudden and alarming peril breathe life
into the spaces round about the human spirit. It
strikes reality into emptiness; form into void;
and gives life unto that which an hour before
was a solitude.

It was but a moment ago when the man upon the
top of the ascending wall saw nothing but bricks
and mortar and human forms, heard nothing but
the shouts of the workmen, the ring of the trowels,
and the creaking of the derrick, when suddenly,
by the slip of his foot he falls, and between the
scaffold and the ground all this sense world dis-
appears, and an unseen world becomes real and

living, the only real and living world before the eyes of the falling man. A single step has taken him out of one world into another! A moment of peril has made vacancy alive, converted void into fullness, nothingness into the only reality!

The lights flash from the cabin, and music's sweet sounds fill all its spaces. Here and there, in groups of two and three, the passengers promenade the deck. Ask these moving forms concerning reality! Old ocean's depths, the solid vessel upon which they stand, yonder distant shore and waiting friends—these things fill human minds, these things move human hearts.

Interrogate these moving forms. What of this vast concave that arches you in, these enveloping spaces through which you drive onward? Empty stretches, vacancy, nothingness. So comes your answer from the heart of the sense-life. But hark! The bell rings out the note of danger! There is a sudden and terrible crash. The ship reels backward, and through the awful gash of the collision the black waters are pouring! What now, where now, is reality? Ah! yonder solid shore, and waiting friends, and ocean's sweeping waves, and iron rib, and oaken plank are seen, are felt no longer, and human spirits are speaking into, actually praying into that which a half-hour ago was emptiness and void.

So the hour of sudden danger waves its wand over vacancy, and forthwith this vacancy lives and is all that does live to the consciousness of the changed man, and the vision of the thrilled human spirit. When peril hangs above it, Jabbok's solitude begins to breathe, to assume form, and the lonely Jacob, before he is aware, is wrestling with it.

Oh! ye who along what ye call your solid streets, and underneath the shadow of your unyielding brick and granite fronts, and before your iron safes, do daily move and stand and bow; Oh! ye who imagine yourselves thus dealing with the only realities of life—I beg you now to stop and remember how soon all these things may become as airy nothings before your changed vision. To-day stop to remember how quickly all reality may be transferred to the realm of the invisible, filled with that which to your present, shallow, sensuous hour seems only so much empty space.

But advancing a step, let me say that the crucial hour breaks upon the sensuous human life in the revelation of a Power hitherto unseen and unfelt—a Power who is King of the invisible realm, Lord and Judge of the human soul.

It is difficult to define personality in so many words. Yet each of us knows what it means, understands well enough how it is separated from being of any other kind. Though the infant life lies a helpless and half-formed thing in the mother's arms, yet you start not back at the sound of your voice, when to this humble, almost inanimate, existence you apply the personal pronoun. You say of the unmoving, scarcely breathing, life, he, she, and when in words to which you expect no reply you make the direct address it is still in the form and by means of the same personal pronoun. But so you do not address Niagara, or the shining star above your head, or the mighty ocean, or the beautiful rose. To none of these do you say, "Thou," as if an answer might come from it to you. So in simplest definition personality is that which we address with the use of the personal pronoun. It is life of our kind—that which may answer back to our voice —a thinking, feeling entity, separated from all other being by the individual consciousness and presided over by the mysterious force of the free and self-directing will.

And in this form, always and for evermore, does the crucial hour of the sense, life photograph the reality of the unseen world. With no wild, unanswering law, with no nameless unpersonal force did Jacob wrestle by Jabbok's ford. Throughout that long eventful night, throughout all the hours of that mysterious and fateful conflict, it was person meeting with person. "There wrestled a man with him until the breaking of the day."

"He said unto him, What is thy name?" "Jacob asked him, and said, Tell me, I pray thee, thy name." Thy name—thy name, so the wrestlers spoke, so they asked of each other. Thou, me—a meeting of persons, a battle of individual and independent wills, a conflict of personal forces the night through.

So ever is it in the crucial hour that breaks over the head of the sense life.

The house is deathly still, and stealing out of the room in which the mute forms of the broken family circle sit together, you softly climb the stairs and stand before the dead body of your boy. If now you kneel by the side of the unmoving form,—and in such an hour the unseen world will be so real to you and so near that you will instinctively do this—if so you bow in worship, the words of your heart will form themselves in no address to impersonal law or force. By the side of your dead child, before such an altar, you will not speak to say, you will not cry out: "Oh, stream of tendency, have pity upon me. Oh, power that makes for righteousness, comfort me! Oh, Great First Cause, give me strength for my weakness, light for my darkness and peace for my aching heart." Not so will your soul speak in such a presence and in such an hour, but instinctively it will break forth in the cry, "O God, have pity, have pity. I did not recognize the Christ Child in the one whom Thou didst send until Thou hadst withdrawn Thy gift. Forgive, forgive my blindness, my earthliness, my brutish sensuousness, for now my heart aches with a measureless grief, and I am Thy child."

So also in the hour of danger. Between the masthead and the deck, between the crashing in of the bullet and the outspeeding of the life, it is unto a person that the human life cries out. All hours of deepest conflict, all hours of danger, of sorrow, and of loss, all hours that break in sifting power upon the head of the sense-life show the reality of the unseen world unto the human spirit in the form of a person. The common, the instinctive ejaculation of the human soul the world over and time through in critical and decisive hours is in the words, "O my God!"

Are not such hours as these as profitable for instruction in spiritual mystery; are they not as reliable in their teaching as are the hours of mirthful jollity, or boastful pride, or over-weening smartness, or festering sin? Nay, are they not better? Do they not stand nearer to, do they not see deeper into, do not they give truer voice, fuller expression to the unchanging and infinite reality?

What then, do you ask, shall be said of those who from out the study, the laboratory, and the philosophical hall give out periphrastic and euphemistic abstractions to take the place of this old concrete word, "God"? This, I think, must be said first of all. Skillful rhetoricians are these men, who under the inspiration of literary taste would fain produce some new and shining phrases; effeminate sons of sturdy fathers often assiduously devoting themselves to the high potencies of a spiritual homeopathy; men playing with phrases; intoxicated with a sense of their own originality; quite beside their true selves; artificial, childishly vain—unspiritual. No doubt it is true that the class whose work it is to put together words for the pages of the review, or for the almost equally ephemeral page of the book, do tire of the old nomenclature. There is, as the great essayist, Foster, pointed out long ago, an aversion on the part of men of literary taste to evangelical religion and if to the thing itself, then of course and also an aversion to the stereotyped phrases by which it is commonly expressed. Then coupled with this aversion is a strange liking for abstract generalities. These commit the writer to nothing, and they have on account of their very indistinctness an impressive echo that is quite pleasing to the literary and philosophical ear. Even Carlyle—rugged prophet as he was—falls a victim to the power of this seduction, and on his pages are found such sonorous phrases as the "Silences," the "Immensities," the "Infinities," the "Eternities." But at the best, even taking in their magniloquent echoes, these phrases are not significant generalizations. At their best they are only glittering generalities, which the human life in its deeper hours puts from it, even as the starving man might thrust from him shining beads and colored glass, crying out, "What need have I of such paltry things as these!"

Behold this written out in letters of light and fire in countless human experiences. The book rests, dust-covered, on the library shelf; the yellow pages of the magazine are going through the mill again, while the author of them both is lying upon the bed of his solitary and judging hour—his heart sobbing out the words, "My God! My

God!" The magazine in the rag-picker's bag, the book forgotten, and the man piteously crying out unto that which he has proved again and again can neither hear nor answer!

By the side of Jabbok's ford, underneath the black cloud of danger, at the end of its power, revealed unto itself, the solitary human spirit calls not unto the Silences or the Eternities, wrestles not with cause, or law, or potency. In the crucial judging, sifting hour, when the unseen becomes real and visible unto the human life, it ever strikes itself into the form of a person, and for this personal Entity there is no other name so good as the old name God—the Infinite One—the Father who is in heaven. Not only so, not only is there no other word so good as this one, but this is also true in the deep and trying hour, when the human spirit, emancipated from the shallow and make-believe conventions of earth, feels itself face to face with Everlasting Reality, it never thinks of naming this Reality by any other name than religion's old word, God.

But again let me ask you to observe that the hour which sifts the sensuous life breaks upon the head of this life in the exposure of its false beauty, in the withering of its false strength, and in the blotting out of its false glory.

"And there wrestled a Man with Jacob until the breaking of the day. And He touched the hollow of his thigh, and Jacob's thigh was out of joint as he wrestled with Him."

Long years before this, in their wrestling match, Jacob was able to throw his brother Esau. In his conflict with Laban also he came off victorious. In both of these encounters he won, as our world uses this word. But now, at length, he has come unto an hour when the glory of these successes withers as the gorgeous sunflower might wither under the breath of the blast furnace : when the heretofore winning Jacob beholds his glory as so much shame and all his meretricious strength in a moment converted into unbeautiful and helpless weakness. No chance for supplanting here. No opportunity for trickery here. No possibility of going in to win upon the low qualities of smartness and shrewdness and cunning. The very qualities that before had been his confidence and his success are now his weakness and his fear.

So, unto the hour of scorching and shriveling, moves every life of sense, every life that has not by thought and purpose penetrated unto that within the veil, every life that has failed to connect its progress, its success and its hope with the everlasting principle of the Divine righteousness.

Take the wild Indian of the wigwam, and set him in the Philosophical Hall: how helpless he seems! how pitiably deficient! how despicably deformed! His fleetness of foot, his sharpness of vision, his strength of limb—all his savage glory are in a moment turned into the contemptible. His glistening beads, his gaudy feathers, his girdle of scalps—all these, his former crown and glory, are now a shame unto him. He has been lifted up into a light that makes a mock of these barbaric ornaments. He stands judged, condemned, in the presence of that which is better and nobler— silenced and ashamed before the power of a higher life. At the touch of this life, his strength shrinks to weakness; in the presence of its superior beauty, his glory withers into shame. So Jacob the wily one, Jacob the supplanter, came into contact with divine and beauteous reality, and at once his strength is out of joint and such an exposure and such a withering await every human life which has not measured its success by the standard of the wider and deeper and eternal world, which is not in consciousness a subject of the everlasting kingdom of God.

Imagine the red Indian before the philosophers. Imagine the low-browed pugilist in the *salon* of culture and beauty. Imagine the able, shrewd,

cunning man of the world lifted up into the at-
mosphere of holiness, into the presence of the
throne that is always white, into the face of the
beautiful God! Oh, what shrinking will such an
hour witness! How its white light will search
out and expose the false beauty! How its dart-
ing fires will scarify the brute strength and consume the shameful glory! The man has been
shrewd, versatile, crafty unto the outer semblance
of success, and the world has glorified his
career. He has won in virtue of the lower qualities of his being, and he has heard himself
praised for these, as for a great success. Now
all at once he is plunged into an hour where all
these qualities show rather as the debasement
of his manhood, and all these victories as so
many defeats of the immortal life! Hitherto he
has fought with his antagonists, using the weapons
of a brutish cunning or a devilish duplicity, and
now in a moment he faces an antagonist who is
Light and in whom is no darkness at all. He
has for long received the honor that cometh from
men. His neighbors have said, "First citizen,"
and taken off their hats; the world has cried
"Millionaire," and bowed down! He himself has
come to regard his life a great success. Now
suddenly he passes into an hour when his money

lifts itself up as the price for which he has bartered things worth more than money, and when his earthly honors disclose themselves as so many weeds of mourning wrapped round a wizened and deformed spirit.

So the hour of judgment breaks upon men ; so it sifts the low smartness and the unworthy success. Oh, what withering of the false bigness will there be in this hour ! Self-revealed, ashamed, self-contemning, the man will shrink into himself, and as a hunted felon dart his terrified gaze in every direction for the corner in which he may hide from the apocalypse of the worthy life and the true glory.

Read once more in the incident of the text that the crucial hour as it breaks upon the head of the sensuous life holds within it the possibility of a new birth—the birth into a new and a higher life.

Out of his mysterious wrestling Jacob comes limping, but he comes forth as a limping prince —his name no longer Jacob, the supplanter, but Israel, spiritual potentate in the kingdom of God. Upon shrunken strength he leans, no longer smart enough to steal from his brother, or to circumvent his uncle, but all this shrinking is of the false bigness, and it is into a weakness, which from the higher level shows as strength. At last Jacob is a true man, at last his life is real. All artifice, all sham, all duplicity, all low cunning have disappeared, consumed by the fire of that awful and glorious hour in which he met with God. Into this hour Jacob went a smart, shrewd, successful commoner, and out of it he comes a true, fair, nobleman. Prostrate in the darkness at Jabbok's ford—conquered by the might of his loving Antagonist—he has heard the voice of this same Antagonist saying unto him, "Stand up, Sir Knight," and he has arisen into place and honor and glory in the family of the great King. Forth from his crucial hour he comes limping—but with a royal limp.

So our world of sham and unreality is full of princes, whose finest decoration is their limping gait. Their outward life has been maimed, but their inward life has been ennobled. On shrunken sinew walk they for the remainder of their earthly days, but from the high table land of immortality God and angels behold in their gait the carriage of the Prince. Into the dark night of fear and of loss, into the darker hour of sorrow and bereavement they have gone, and, after long wrestling hours with the living and the true One, they themselves have come forth true, and alive with the life of God. The sifting hour of the deep experience has smitten them down into the consciousness of weakness, into the consciousness of shame, but their consternation and their suffering have been the travail pains of a new birth. Unto each one of them also has the great King spoken to say, "Stand up, Sir Knight," and they have stood up—out of their low smartness, out of their shrewd self-seeking, out of their self-complacency, out of the mire of their success—stood up new men and true! Oh, ye who have so won, even through your defeat, rejoice in this defeat. Oh, ye who have wrestled in the dark hours unto your utter exhaustion, give thanks for the surrender that was forced upon you! Oh, ye who with limping gait and straitened outward life walk forward unto the eternities, rejoice in this, that the inward life has been purified, that the spirit has been ennobled, and that in God's sight ye do now walk as princes.

So, in outline, is drawn in the incident of the text, the hour which is to sift the sensuous life. Not altogether fascinating is it, I know, in many of our earthly, animal days to contemplate it. We are such creatures of flesh and blood, so wrapped

round with the material and the sensuous, so
dominated by the conventions of a disordered
world that we shrink back from the nakedness, the
exposure threatened by unpitying reality and the
unveiled God. But since we do not stay here, but
move swiftly forward into the sifting hour, it would
seem the part of wisdom for us, as it is the gra-
cious opportunity of the present day, to prepare
ourselves for it.

This can be done, first of all, by familiarizing
ourselves with the idea of the world to come.
Definite knowledge of facts, I know, is not possible here, but spiritual impression is. If you
will walk with earth's new man from the hour
in which, as with the innocent wonder of childhood, He lifts up the interrogation, " Wist ye not
that I must be about My Father's business ?"
until in the gloaming of His earthly day you shall
hear Him exclaim, " I have finished the work which
Thou gavest Me to do," you will have impressed
upon you the fact that this is not the only world
to which man belongs ; you will come to feel the
powers of an unseen world—to taste these powers,
even as the river tastes the saltness of the sea, far
up its earthly banks.

Then there is a second element of preparation
within your reach, even acquaintance with God.

Here again I know human vision is blind and human reason is impotent. But the Divine Man here again is Helper and Saviour. "No man hath seen God at any time; the only begotten Son, which is in the bosom of the Father, He hath declared Him." "In the beginning was the Word, and the Word was with God, and the Word was God. . . And the Word was made flesh, and dwelt among us." "He that hath seen Me hath seen the Father."

So if you will become familiar with the Christ—and this is your privilege—you will not be afraid nor ashamed when you are swept forward into the presence of Him, upon whose image, manifest in human form, you have learned to look.

Then there remains for you this third step of preparation, the keeping ever before you in plainest view, the true standard of the real beauty and the true glory of rational life. Here also He, who is the Head of the new humanity, waits upon your necessity, offers Himself unto you as Saviour. The world has never found any "fault in Him." He is the Model, the perfect Man. He will show you, if you are willing to look, if you wish to learn what you ought to be, and what you may become.

These three ideas, Christ the revealer of God,

Christ the minister plenipotentiary from the world that is to come unto the world that now is, Christ the image of the true man—by the power of these great truths, faithfully used, you may fashion for yourself a life which no night of earth's darkness, and no hour of future surprise, shall have power to terrify, to wound, or to rob.

VIII

TWO GREAT DEEPS

VIII

TWO GREAT DEEPS

"Thy judgments are a great deep."—PSALM xxxvi : 6.

IN the language of the Bible, the judgments of God are the purposes of the Divine will taking shape in human history, the self-manifestations of the Infinite under the conditions of time and space. The great deep, also another common Bible phrase, is the wide blue sea, mightiest of God's earthly creatures, that forever rolls and tosses within the sight of man. So by the words of the text are we to-day invited to take our stand upon its beach, and, while we look out upon the great ocean, learn something of Him of whom it is declared, " Thy way is in the sea, and Thy path in the great waters."

The first and most evident attribute of the great deep is its unresting action, the never-ceasing character of its motion. At times, when spending the sacred day in the country, it has seemed to me as if the quiet of earth's sweet rest day had fallen upon nature as well as upon the souls of

men. The breezes seemed to stir the leaves with
a gentler motion. The supporting accompani-
ment of animate life, which, like the ticking of the
clock, is unheard in common hours, came into
notice, and seemed a special orchestra prepared
with tender and minor strains for the worship of
the solemn hours, and even the chattering brooks,
like noisy children who have been rebuked by the
falling of a sudden calm upon their elders about
them, seemed to moderate their joy and glide in
softer murmurs over the ripples in their gleaming
pathway. But the ocean knows no Sabbath, no
rest day, no hour of peaceful quiet. It is the
troubled sea that cannot rest. When you lay
yourself down upon your bed at night the plash-
ing of the waves upon the beach tells you that
there is no sleep for them, and if you awaken at
dead of night the deep undertone of their motion
reports itself at once to your opening ears, and in
the morning, as you stand upon the new-made
beach, you read the proof that there is no period
of inaction in the life of the great deep; that while
earth and man may rest and sleep, the wide blue
sea, like its great Creator, fainteth not, neither is
weary. Now, as summer suns have begun to
wheel their higher circles in the heavens, throwing
down their furnace flames upon the head of man

and beast, there shall flock to old ocean's side a great company of those who for another year have worked and rested, have lain down and risen up, and the first sight that they shall look upon as the whitened beach lifts itself again into view will be the advancing and receding waves, the same unchanged motions, the same undiminished restlessness of the years before. Long after these children of the summer excursion have visited the ocean for the last time, and have laid themselves down in the silence of the sleep that knows no waking, the same waves that they are looking upon to-day shall come and go, shall hurry in and hurry out, shall toss and sport themselves in the same unceasing and unwearied movements with which they greeted and pleased the eyes and the ears of visitors of other days and of past generations.

Turn now from the symbol unto that which is symbolized, from the great deep unto Him who holds its mighty masses in the hollow of His hand. The Infinite mind and will are necessarily and eternally active. In the realm of creation, of providence, and of grace there is no resting of the purpose of Deity, no slumbering of the judgments of the Almighty. Individual development, world-change, world-progress, the onsweeping life of universal nature, these all proclaim the ceaseless activity, the continuous self-manifestation of Him, who is in all, and through all, the alone fountain of all force, the impulse of all movement, the soul of all life.   Consider this activity as it has been revealed unto the children of men in this earth province of the universal empire.

Under the brooding of the Divine Spirit upon the formless waste, the waters that were under the firmament drew themselves away from the waters which were above the firmament—then earth's fire-mist grew dense, then denser still ; then light flashed in upon the darkness, order spoke unto confusion—five mighty days lifted up their finished work while they listened for the acceptance and approval of the Divine Architect, given out in the words, " It is very good " ; and then a sixth day came—also one of the great thousand-year days of the Lord,—and the earth rolled forth into space the finished dwelling-place of man !

Since that far-off period of creation's power there has been no stopping, no rest within this earth of ours.   By day and by night, around its own axis, around the sun, and with sun and planet and satellite forward around some far-off and mysterious center, it has wheeled onward through the centuries—through the centuries which are only so many pendulum beats of its mighty life, and inconceivable orbit. Upon its surface, too, all is motion, and change, and progress. Its seasons flow onward in a current that knows no slackening. Its rivers run to the sea with a music that never intermits. Its clouds are yearly transformed into bread for its millions of pilgrim-pensioners. Its valleys are being filled ; its mountains leveled. Men are multiplying upon its surface and within its graves. Knowledge is increasing ; civilization is advancing ; art and science are conquering new fields and winning new trophies—the past is evermore forgotten, and under the superintendence of some mighty power, our earth and all that it contains goes spinning down the grooves of time, taking hold of an orbit that no human eye may see and no human intelligence may measure.

So also and as wonderful are the activity and progress of the moral realm. In the soundless depths of a past eternity the purpose of redemption was fashioned. Time brought forth the theater of its manifestation, and the object of its wondrous power. Since the first day of human history, where has there been shown any sign of end or rest ? The gloaming of the morning has ever been lifting itself up into the light of a more perfect day. Promise has ripened into fulfillment ;

type has been lost in anti-type. The church of a family has widened into the church of a nation, and this through centuries of discipline and of growth has broadened into the church of a world, and this world-church, with the growth of centuries in her stature, lifts herself up before us to-day, the dew of youth sparkling upon her beautiful garments and the light of hope flushing her fair face as she turns her eyes upon the misty stretches of humanity's mighty future. There is no weakening of her faith, no wasting of her power. Daily is she laying the hand of her guidance upon some new world-force, stirring the hearts of men with the influence of some higher motive and some sweeter hope ; by one incline after another lifting the world up unto higher and yet higher table-lands of thought, of purpose, and of being. Through the shaking of the nations, through and over the oppositions of men, by the sweet breath of human love, by the harsh and strident gale of human wrath, is the ever-enlarging hope of the new humanity which is in and through Christ Jesus, being swept forward, and of rest, of harbor, of anchorage there is yet no sign. What are all these movements, these changes, this progress, but the self-manifestation of the Infinite, the birth into time, and human history of the purposes of His immutable and omnipotent will.

Yet what is our earth? A point in infinite space. What is time with its circling ages? A point in infinite duration. All the wonders, all the changes, the multiplied, the progressive, the endless movements of human history, what are these all but the outworking, the manifestation of the infinite purpose in a moment of eternity and in point of immensity? Oh, the glories which must rise before the eye that can sweep the universe of space and duration! Oh, the waves which before such a vision must lift themselves up and sweep across the mighty expanse! Oh, the sublime, the awful gulf current which such observation must note, setting its course toward, cutting its way through the ages " unto that far-off divine event to which the whole creation moves "! Oh, the overwhelming glory of the final end, forever unapproached, forever unapproachable! Oh, the glory of the ever-living God! " Thy judgments are a great deep."

But the ocean is not only unceasing in its activity, but it is sublimely irresistible in the mightiness of its power.

Even when the sea is placid, our minds instinctively clothe it with majestic and measureless force. In the low plash of the sunlit waves we hear disguised the same voice that boomed artillery-like through the night time of fear. We watch the ocean, even in its hours of play, with much the same feeling that we look upon the sporting of the wild beast, not knowing how soon its sport may give place to rage, and its harmless activity change to a superhuman destructiveness. But while the ocean always and everywhere impresses the human mind with the idea of unlimited power, there are times and seasons in its life when its majestic force comes out in bolder form and thrills us with a more awesome wonder. When, for illustration, turning as some restless monster from one side to the other, he begins to push his mighty masses in upon the land, what power can oppose his progress or bid back his on-sweeping billows? Slowly and majestically turn his quickened depths toward the land; higher and higher rises each successive wave; farther and still farther up upon the shore he throws his tidal fullness, and then, while we look, he reverses the motion of his liquid masses, and with an energy that none can hinder, and with a retreat that no power may cut off, rolls them back again into the hollow of the great deep.

The storm is even a grander exhibition of

the ocean's power than the tide. When the
heavens grow black above his uneasy masses, and
lurid lightning cuts this blackness into horrible
gashes; when the winds, as if let loose from the
gates of hell, whip into foam the sweeping billows
until one would think the deep were hoary; when
there succeeds to the momentary calm, which is
itself frightful, the first burst of the hurricane, and
to that low moaning and indistinct muttering of
mighty wrath, the thunder of the wild billows
coming forth rank after rank from their garrison
in the deep; when these voices are all answered
back by the angry voices of the sky; when the
deep below calls unto the deep above, then how
puny seems the noblest conception of human
power—how majestically terrible the aroused
might of the great ocean!

With this sight before your eyes, turn unto that
of which it is the symbol.

"The voice of the Lord is upon the waters . . .
which stilleth the noise of the seas, the noise of
their waves, and the tumult of the people."

The Divine purposes as they manifest themselves in human history are not only irresistible,
but they move on to their end through the use of
the humblest instrumentalities, through agencies
and influences which seem contemptible to hu-

man eyes. This is the grandest conceivable exhibition of measureless force. When power can afford to be parsimonious of her resources; when she can accomplish her ends through the help of the most humble allies, then it is that she arrays herself in her most glorious apparel and lifts to her head her most resplendent crown.

Of such exhibitions of power the history of our world is full. When their Divine Leader in the olden day would, for His chosen people, conquer the menacing host of the Midianites, He sends against them, not the thirty thousand which were at His command, but three hundred only; He smites the giant of Gath with a pebble from a stripling's sling; scatters an army by the flash of a lamp and the blare of a trumpet; revolutionizes the world by twelve fishermen; reforms the church by a single-handed monk as against the power of pope and prince and emperor; and through the centuries, by means of the "foolishness of preaching," carries forward a work over which the celestial hierarchies bend in liveliest interest, and by which are shaped the fate of nations and the history of the world. Pictures these, all of them, of the ineffable ease with which the purposes of the Divine administration work unto their appointed end in the development of our race. Then even beyond this wondrous exhibition reaches the resplendent fullness of their matchless and measureless power. Not only do they employ forces scorned of human judgment, but they make readiest use of the oppositions of men to accomplish their designs.

Look back upon old Babel. "Unto consolidation, unto centralization, unto unity let it work, cried the voice of the human builders." He that sitteth in the heavens heard, and from His throne came forth this response unto the children of men: "The Divine purpose is to scatter men over the face of the earth, and your work will lend itself readily to this end." And what did history write down? Why, Babel,—that is, dispersion. So we read unto this day.

Cast a glance into ancient Egypt. Political wisdom, the power of a despotic throne, declares the decree and every man-child of the Israelites is doomed. But the more the people were oppressed, the more they multiplied and grew. Nay, more! The very measure that was designed to render their slavery perpetual threw into the court of Pharaoh, there to be trained in all the wisdom of Egypt, the deliverer of the bondsmen. As though it were not enough for the Divine purpose to accomplish deliverance, it causes the taskmasters with their own hands to break the fetters they had forged, compels the house of Pharaoh to nourish and to educate a Moses. " He that sitteth in the heavens shall laugh."

Hear the echoes of this same laugh in the western world and in our own day, where insatiate ambition of American slavery for extension and defense was turned into the great emancipation measure of the nineteenth century. But take the supreme illustration, and let it suffice for all. With wicked hands men seized and crucified heaven's well-beloved and earth's fairest Son. Yes! but Pilate, with a hand that he might not stay, was obliged to reach forth and write the word " King " over the head of the dying Jesus; Joseph's sepulcher gave up to the world an immortal name and an endless power; and even the dumb cross, which had been unwittingly the agent of death, became a thing of life, the standard of an ever-increasing and invincible host. He who was cut off out of the land without issue and without generation, now counts His children by the thousands in every land that is visited by the sun. The Man of sorrows and of death has become the joy and the life of a world. " Thy judgments, O God, are a great deep."

A third characteristic of the great deep is the

order that controls all its unceasing movements, that directs and tethers all the outreachings of its mighty power. This would not appear to the observer who should for the first time stand upon its shores. To such an one the rise and fall of its mighty waves, the incoming and the outgoing of its tidal masses would indicate no order and voice no law. But if such an observer should return day after day, and year after year, to look with reason's eye upon the liquid continent, he would surely be forced to the conclusion that underneath the apparent lawlessness that first impressed him there is some regulative force governing the seemingly capricious movements, and dictating both certainty and uniformity to all the manifestations of their mighty life. Such an one would be sure to hear, breaking forth from the vast and weltering plain before him, the words of this mysterious voice: "Thus far shalt thou go, and no farther: and here shall thy proud waves be stayed." As a matter of fact, men have stood now for centuries looking out from ocean's shore, and with what result? The table of the tidal movements can now be written down years before their occurrence; the equatorial and polar currents can now be mapped, and the racing gulf streams, and the yearly tide-rises, and the mysterious undertows, these all can be charted for the guidance of the adventurous voyager.

We who by the voice of the text to-day are invited unto ocean's beach to learn our lesson, are thus warranted in attributing a similar order to the judgments of the Almighty, to the purposes of the overruling Power, as these take hold of and manifest themselves in the affairs of our disordered world. I know that the philosophy of history is yet but poorly understood and imperfectly written. Historians stand upon the mighty beach of our world's life, and in the activity of its great forces see nothing but so much confused and aimless motion; so much result and effect of human passion and human greed; so much outwriting of the uncontrolled desires of human hearts and the ungoverned purposes of the human will. Hence and through all the centuries they have been lifting up this voice: "Where is the promise of His coming? for since the fathers fell asleep, all things continue as they were from the beginning of the creation."

But this is only because these observers have not stood long enough upon the world-encircling beach, or long enough with eyes opened by the touch of the Divine Spirit, marked down the movements upon which they looked. This is because the eye which sees here is the one that opened in its little cradle but yesterday; because the human mind finite, and infantile, has here to do with the infinite, with the great immeasurable days of the Lord. So centuries ago, the astronomer, directing his gaze to yonder star, cried out, " It does not move; the shining point is a fixed one in the mighty star field." But now, to-day, the astronomer directs his telescopic vision unto the same star, and this is the voice that we hear: "Ah, it has moved! The glittering point was not a fixed diamond pinned upon the bosom of the night." The first observer was mistaken because he looked upon a sun the seconds of whose mighty orbit were so many of earth's centuries; he drew a false conclusion because there was not time enough between his cradle and his grave for him to learn the stupendous truth.

So are we bidden, by the analogy of the text, to believe it is with the gulf stream of the Divine purpose in the ocean of time. Through the ages one increasing purpose runs, and with unresting and invincible force is sweeping onward to the end of universal order and everlasting righteousness. That the Divine purpose in human history does more in this direction, that it has so moved, this year of our Lord nineteen hundred and three bears unmistakable and convincing witness. America is better than the republic whose ashes are strewn on the banks of the Tiber—better as Rome was better than the dynasties that rose and fell to the music of the Euphrates and the Tigris. The current of the overruling purpose has swept our world forward—forward unto a larger knowledge and a wider wisdom—forward unto a nobler freedom and a higher civilization—forward unto a larger type of the individual man and a grander form of the nation—forward unto a fuller understanding and a more abounding enjoyment of the teaching and the promise of the Cross.

No doubt there are isolated events, anomalous plans, great crises and centuries in our world's life which seem to be so many retrograde currents. So there are in the arctic region and upon the bosom of the current that is setting toward the equator, surface waves which flow toward the pole. There is upon the bosom of the incoming tide a multitude of wavelets whose movement is away from the shore. Granted all this— yet shall the equator bathe itself in the waters that have poured from the northern sea and the continent receive upon its majestic front the far-resounding dash of the tidal wave. So, taught by the intuition of the soul and by the past progress of the human race, as well as by the declared analogy of the text, must we not say that the current of human history shall yet lift itself up into and break upon the front of the great white throne in the exulting joy of this millennial chorus : " The kingdoms of this world are become the kingdoms of our Lord, and of His Christ; and He shall reign for ever and ever." So shall order grow out of that which we now deem confusion, and so shall the judgments of the Infinite One—now a great and weltering maze before the eyes of men—stretch themselves out as a sea of glass, mirrored in which the universe shall read for evermore the grace and the glory, the wisdom and the power of Him who is the Creator of worlds, the Father of men, and the King of all our earth.

Thus standing by invitation of the text upon the beach of the deep blue sea, have we learned the lesson given unto us,—unresting action, immeasurable power, immutable order. And how wonderfully majestic and sublime is the creation of the Almighty that to-day lifts up before us these glorious attributes! If you will open your eyes, you will see the ocean in uniform of blue and white flowing unto every shore; if you will open your ears, you will catch the music of its perpetual thunder as it girdles the globe, and rises in mighty chorus to the skies. In its embrace the opposite poles of earth are in contact; great islands are only so many phosphorescent atoms quivering in its waters, and whole continents are but the jewels that it wears upon its broad bosom.

But there is yet a mightier sea than earth's great ocean. It is the great deep of the Divine judgments, the great deep of the self-manifestations of the Infinite. On its broad surface glittering constellations are the phosphorescent light, and uncounted systems of suns and of worlds, the jewels with which its raiment sparkles. Out yonder to Sirius, from which the swift-darting light comes wearily after the lapse of centuries— out yonder to the unresolved star dust of the Milky Way, where even imagination grows sick with its awful flight—unto those distant shores I can see the waters of this mighty deep flowing, and while I listen I can hear their echoes as in sublime doxology they rise to the Infinite Throne. A sea whose waters lave every shore within this boundless universe—this is the great deep of the Divine judgments. A sea of infinity pouring itself round immensity—this is the self-manifestation of the Infinite, this the propulsive energy and the controlling force of the Divine purpose.

Upon this great deep you are embarked—a voyager whether you will or no. Is not this true? Are you not so embarked? By all the power that you possess can you abrogate your gift of life, or even reverse the motion of your being? Have you any hand of choice or might to expunge or rewrite the decree which declares that you shall go forward whither you know not, try a course that you cannot map down? Surely you are embarked as a voyager whether you will or no.

What shall be your preparations, your outfit, for this mysterious and adventurous voyage? I can see the young man, resplendent in the glory that his tailor has loaned him, turning his feathery yacht, without compass or anchor, without strength of spar or width of beam, into the mighty billows and raging storms of the broad Atlantic. The sight is not a pleasant one. It is such a mockery of reality. It is such a travesty upon human wisdom and human strength.

So I can see a human life swept forward over a deep that it cannot fathom, into storms that it cannot resist, unto a harbor that it cannot foresee, and all the while self-confident, self-complacent, irreverent, prayerless, not even serious. This also is a pitiful spectacle. It jars upon reason. It is

12

so out of keeping with the nature of things. It is such a pathetic and needless exposure of the weak and fearing spirit of a man. Against this sense-madness lovingly and earnestly I warn you to-day.

The outfit which you, my fellow-man, need for your adventurous voyage is not the natty costume of any one of this world's fashions, but the old and simple garment of a reverent faith. That which is consonant with your being, and suited to your necessities beyond even the power of your imagination to perfect it, is the child-heart within you, taking hold of the Infinite Father above you, reaching out unto Him who is wise to direct, pitiful to succor, and almighty to save—director of currents—ruler of waves—master of storms.

So equipped with this filial spirit, you will be able to pass through all dark days in calmness and with courage, and when the hour of storm and stress shall break, you will be prepared to sing your every fear to sleep with the sweet lullaby of this beautiful and blessed trust :—

> For, though from out our bourne of time and place
> The flood may bear me far,
> I hope to see my Pilot face to face
> When I have crossed the bar.

Lightning Source UK Ltd.
Milton Keynes UK
UKHW020648241218
334505UK00007B/95/P